MACMILLAN
MUSIC and YOU

MACMILLAN
MUSIC and YOU

Barbara Staton, Senior Author
Merrill Staton, Senior Author
Marilyn Davidson
Phyllis Kaplan

Macmillan Publishing Company
New York

Collier Macmillan Publishers
London

ACKNOWLEDGMENTS

Grateful acknowledgment is given to the following authors and publishers. In the case of some songs and poems for which acknowledgment is not given, we have earnestly endeavored to find the original source and to procure permission for their use, but without success. Extensive research failed to locate the author and/or copyright holder.

Fran Smartt Addicott for *The Train*. Reprinted by permission of Fran Smartt Addicott, Memphis, TN.

Alfred Publishing Co., Inc. for *Nature's Sweet Endless Song*, music and lyrics by Hap Palmer from HAP PALMER FAVORITES, published in 1981. Used by permission of the publisher, Alfred Publishing Co., Inc.

Behrman House for *Hanan and Aliza* by H. C. and F. Minkoff from THE NEW JEWISH SONG BOOK by Harry Coopersmith, 1965. Used by permission.

Belwin Mills for *Ebeneezer Sneezer* from SONGS FOR OUR SMALL WORLD by Lynn Freeman Olson. Copyright © 1968 by Schmitt Music Center. Reprinted by permission of Belwin Mills Publishing Corp. All rights reserved. *Never Sleep Late Anymore* by George Winston, compiled by Robert Kensey. © 1972 by Belwin Mills Publishing Corp. International copyright secured. All rights reserved.

Bowmar for *Japanese Rain Song* from SING A SONG by McLaughlin and Wood. Reprinted by permission of Bowmar, Division of McGraw-Hill School Division.

Canadian Museum of Civilization for *Oh! The Pretty Butterflies*, music only, reprinted courtesy of the Canadian Museum of Civilization.

Wayne Chadwick for *April Fool's Day*. Used by permission of the composer.

Cherry Lane Music for *The Marvelous Toy* by Tom Paxton from SONGS FOR A NEW GENERATION. Copyright © 1961, 1964 Cherry Lane Music Publishing Co., Inc. All rights reserved. Used by permission; *The Garden Song* by David Mallet. Copyright © 1975 Cherry Lane Music Publishing Co., Inc. All rights reserved. Used by permission.

Crown Publishers for *Shepherd, Shepherd* reprinted from AMERICAN NEGRO SONGS AND SPIRITUALS by John W. Work. Copyright © 1968 by Crown Publishers, Inc. Used by permission of Crown Publishers, Inc.

Doubleday for *October* by Rose Fyleman from GAY GO UP. Copyright © 1929, 1930 by Doubleday & Company, Inc. Reprinted by permission of the publisher.

Fideree Music Company for *Pity the Poor Patat* by Josef Marais. Copyright © 1946 and 1956.

Mark Foster Music Company for *Up and Down* from KODÁLY APPROACH. Used by permission of Mark Foster Music Co.

Geordie Music Publishing, Inc. for *Skin and Bones* by Jean Ritchie. Copyright © 1952 Jean Ritchie, Geordie Music Publishing Co.

Evelyn Hunt Harris for *The Valentine* (in book titled *My Valentine*) from MUSIC NOW AND LONG AGO. Reprinted by permission of Evelyn Hunt Harris.

D. C. Heath for *Trains at Night* by Francis M. Frost from THE PACKET. By permission of D. C. Heath and Company.

Constance B. Heidt for *Thanksgiving* from THE BROOKSIDE SONGBOOK. Copyright © 1983—Brookside Songbook.

John Horman for *I Am a Leprechaun*; the musical *Stone Soup*; *Welcome Friends* and *Friendship Canon*. All works copyright © John Horman, 1001 Spring Street, Silver Spring, MD 20910.

Alan Lomax for *In Good Old Colony Times*, piano arrangement by Don Banks, from THE FOLKSONGS OF NORTH AMERICA. Published by Doubleday in 1960.

MMB Music, Inc. for *Circle 'Round the Zero* from CIRCLE 'ROUND THE ZERO: PLAY CHANTS AND SINGING GAMES OF CITY CHILDREN by Maureen Kenney. Copyright © 1983 MMB Music, Inc. Used by permission. Unauthorized Reproduction Prohibited.

Macmillan Publishing Co. for *Snow* by Elizabeth Coatsworth from SING A SONG OF SEASONS by Sara & John Brewton. Reprinted by permission of Macmillan Publishing Company. Copyright © 1948 by Macmillan Publishing Company, renewed 1976 by Elizabeth Coatsworth Beston.

Memphis Musicraft Publications for *Lullaby* by Carole King from RECORDER ROUTES, I; *Halloween Night* by Doris Parker from HOLIDAYS, 21 FESTIVE ARRANGEMENTS FOR UNCHANGED VOICES AND ORFF INSTRUMENTS, Copyright © 1980 Memphis Musicraft Publications, 3149 Southern Ave., Memphis, TN 38111. Used by permission.

Macmillan Publishing Company
866 Third Avenue
New York, N.Y. 10022
Collier Macmillan Canada, Inc.

Printed in the United States of America

ISBN: 0-02-293350-6
12 11 10

Mona Lowe and MM Publications for *Tue, Tue* from SINGING GAMES FROM GHANA by Mona Lowe, Yucca Valley, CA.

William Morrow Co., Inc. for *The First Thanksgiving* from IT'S THANKSGIVING by Jack Prelutsky. Copyright © 1982 by Jack Prelutsky. Used by permission of Greenwillow Books (a Division of William Morrow & Company).

Oxford University Press for *If All Men Would Live as Brothers* by Michael Lane. From EARS AND EYES 4 by Jack Dobbs, Roger Fiske, and Michael Lane. © Oxford University Press, England 1979. Reprinted by permission.

Prentice-Hall for *Telehone Song* from THE KODÁLY CONTEXT: CREATING AN ENVIRONMENT FOR MUSICAL LEARNING by Lois Choksy, 1981. Reproduced by permission of Prentice-Hall, Inc., Englewood Cliffs, N.J.

Carroll Rinehart for the music to *Which Is the Way to London Town?*. Reprinted by permission of the composer.

Rockhaven Music for *Tongue-Twister Canon, My Valentine, Mama Paquita, Tinga Layo, Pat-a-Pan.* Copyright © 1986 and 1987.

Carmen Roy for English words of *Oh! The Pretty Butterflies*, from *Saint-Pierre and Miquelon*, Bulletin 182, Anthropological Series 56. Ottawa: National Museum of Canada, 1962, page 165.

Shawnee Press, Inc. for *Song of the Dragon* from FUN, FOOD AND FESTIVALS by Kathryn G. Obenshain, Alice D. Walker and Joyce Merman. Copyright © 1978 Shawnee Press, Inc., Delaware Water Gap, PA 18327. All rights reserved.

The Society of Authors for *October* by Rose Fyleman. The Society of Authors as the literary representative of the Estate of Rose Fyleman.

Stormking Music Inc. for *Grizzly Bear*, arrangement by Andrew B. Crane. Copyright © 1965 by Stormking Music Inc. Used by permission.

David and Phyllis Stycos for *Christmas Is Joy*. Used with permission of David and Phyllis Stycos, Kalamazoo, Mich.

Warner Brothers Inc. for *High Is Better Than Low* by Howard Dietz and Arthur Schwartz. Copyright © 1963 Warner Brothers Inc. All rights reserved. Used by permission.

Jackie Weissman for *Sing About Martin* from INSTRUCTOR MAGAZINE, January 1984. Reprinted by permission of Jackie Weissman.

Some line drawings of musical instruments reprinted by permission of Harvard University Press from NEW HARVARD DICTIONARY OF MUSIC by Don M. Randel. Copyright 1987 by the President and Fellows of Harvard College.

PHOTO CREDITS:

© CLARA AICH: 34, 35, 57, 113, 180R, 187. ART RESOURCE, NY: The Bridgeman Art Library, 64; Giraudon, 87, 106, 119; Kavaler, 94; Scala/ARS/SPADEM, 173. THE BETTMAN ARCHIVE: 60. BLACK STAR: B & C. Alexander 154; C. Ray Moore, 108. WOODFIN CAMP & ASSOCIATES: Marc & Evelyne Bernheim, 174-5C, 203L; Michal Heron, 21TR; George P. Koshollek, 175R; Horst Munzig, 181TL; William Strode, 90-1C. Courtesy, CENTER FOR U.S.-CHINA ARTS EXCHANGE: Photo by Joe Pineiro, Performed by Wu Wenguang, 202. DPI: © Randy Bishop, 157. LEO DEWYS: David Burnett, 123R. © MARJORY DRESSLER: 185, 196. DRK PHOTO: N.H. (Dan) Cheatham, 123C; Stephen J. Krasemann, 10, 91C; Wayne Lankinen, 65C; Tom A. Schneider, 142TL. FOUR BY FIVE: 164, both. FOLIO, INC.: E.R. Degginger, 91TR. Copyright © 1985 Grandma Moses Properties Co., NY: 193. FPG INTERNATIONAL: Dick Luria, 95. SOLOMON R. GUGGENHEIM MUSEUM, NY: Gift, Solomon R. Guggenheim, 1937, Photo: David Heald, 117T. Collection HAMPTON UNIVERSITY MUSEUM, Hampton, VA: Photo by Mike Fischer, 25. HISTORICAL PICTURES SERVICES: 125. THE IMAGE BANK: Ernest Braun, 20-1C; G. Colliva, 114; Hans-Pete Dinke, 14-3C; Steve Dunwell, 22; Garry Gay, 201; Lou Jones, 49TR; Don Klumpp, 181R; Barbara Kreye, 21R; Elyse Lewin, 65R; Peter Miller, 42; Al Satterwhite, 181 BL; Alvis Upitis, 1TC; Anne van der Vaeren, 174T; John Wagner, Jr., 33. MANHATTAN VIEWS INC.: Gerry Ellis, 205C. THE METROPOLITAN MUSEUM OF ART, NY: Excavations of The Metropolitan Museum of Art, Rogers Fund, 1931 (31.3.98), 180; Gift of John M. Crawford, Jr., 1984 (1984.274), 190; John M. Crawford, Jr., Collection, Purchase, Douglas Dillon Gift, 1981 (1981.278), 190-1; Gift of the Dillon Fund, 1973 (1973.120.6, Detail #5), 191. © LAWRENCE MIGDALE: 122-3TC. © WILLIAM MILLS, Montgomery County Public School System: 83. MUSÉES ROYAUX DES BEAUX ARTS DE BELGIQUE, Brussels: 114B. MUSEUM OF FINE ARTS, Boston: Bequest of Mrs. Edward Jackson Holmes, Edward Jackson Homes Collection, 3; Bequest of Maxim Karolik, 27. ODYSSEY PRODUCTIONS: Robert Frerck, 74R. THE PHILLIPS COLLECTION, Washington, DC, 23, 127. © GEORGE PICKOW: 46, 47, 49T, 54, 55. RAINDOW: Coco McCoy, 143R. © HENRY RIES: 198. S.F. PHOTO NETWORK: René de la Briandais, 166TL, TR, 203R; John Sievert, 49TL. © VICTORIA BELLER SMITH: 13, 70, 71C, 76, 86, 93, 99, 100, 101, 104, 112, 116, 126, 135, 138, 146, 147, 153, 159, 166C, 186, 188, 199. SMITHSONIAN INSTITUTION, Washington, DC, 51. TOM STACK & ASSOCIATES: Tom Stack, 45. Courtesy, STEINWAY & SONS: 37. THE STOCK MARKET: Jon Feingersh, x; Harvey Lloyd, 122; Roy Morsh, 90, 143TC; Gabe Palmer, 44-5TC; Claudia Parks, 20TL; Richard Steedman, 64-5T, 73, 205B; Bo Zaunders, 45R. TAURUS PHOTOS INC.: Ronald F. Thomas, 205T. © JOHN TERHUNE: 117B. U.S. NAVY: 5. Joseph Viesti: 1R. WHEELER PICTURES: John Dominis, 74L, 167, 175TC; Paul Solomon, x-1TC.

AUTHORS

Barbara Staton has taught music at all levels, kindergarten through college, and for eight years was music television teacher for the State of Georgia. She is author of a four-volume series of books and records designed to teach music concepts through movement. She holds a B.S. degree in Music Education and an M.A. in Dance and Related Arts. Mrs. Staton has written numerous songs for television and recordings and is a composer member of ASCAP.

Dr. Merrill Staton earned his M.A. and Ed.D. degrees from Teachers College, Columbia University, and is nationally known as a music educator, choral conductor, singer, composer and record producer. He has been music director and has conducted the Merrill Staton Voices on many network TV series and recordings. Dr. Staton has been a leader in the field of music education for the past twenty-five years, and pioneered the use of children's voices on recordings for education.

Marilyn Davidson teaches elementary general music in Pequannock, New Jersey. She also teaches graduate summer courses in music education at Potsdam University of New York; the Hartt School of Music at the University of Hartford in West Hartford, Connecticut; and Teachers College, Columbia University, in New York City. Her teaching experience spans twenty-eight years at all levels.

Dr. Phyllis Kaplan received her Ph.D. in Music Education from the University of Michigan. She has taught in the Ohio public schools and at Kent State and Penn State Universities. She has served on the MENC National Committee on Music Education for Handicapped Learners. Currently, she is Coordinator of Elementary General Music for the Montgomery County Public Schools, Rockville, Maryland. She is on the Music Educators Journal editorial board.

SPECIAL CONTRIBUTORS

Dr. Betty Atterbury
Mainstreaming

Marshia Beck
Movement

Mary Frances Early
Black American Music

Joan Gregoryk
Vocal Development

János Horváth
Kodály

Virginia Mead
Dalcroze

Mollie Tower
Listening Selections

CONSULTANTS AND CONTRIBUTING WRITERS

Dr. Betty Atterbury, University of Southern Maine, Gorham, Maine ● **Marshia Beck,** Holy Names College, Oakland, California ● **Diane Bennette,** Bergenfield Public Schools, Bergenfield, New Jersey ● **Dr. Joyce Boorman,** University of Alberta, Edmonton, Alberta, Canada ● **Teri Burdette,** Barnsley Elementary, Rockville, Maryland ● **Dr. Robert A. Duke,** University of Texas, Austin, Texas ● **Mary Frances Early,** Atlanta Public Schools, Atlanta, Georgia ● **Nancy Ferguson,** Memphis Public Schools, Memphis, Tennessee ● **Diane Fogler,** Rockaway Township Public Schools, Rockaway, New Jersey ● **Joan Gregoryk,** Chevy Chase Elementary, Chevy Chase, Maryland ● **János Horváth,** University of Calgary, Calgary, Alberta, Canada ● **Dr. Judith A. Jellison,** University of Texas, Austin, Texas ● **Dr. JaFran Jones,** Bowling Green State University, Bowling Green, Ohio ● **James Kenwood,** Howe Avenue Elementary, Sacramento, California ● **Tom Kosmala,** Pittsburgh Public Schools, Pittsburgh, Pennsylvania ● **Virginia Mead,** Kent State University, Kent, Ohio ● **Belle San Miguel-Ortiz,** San Antonio Independent School District, San Antonio, Texas ● **Jane Pippart,** Lancaster Public Schools, Lancaster, Pennsylvania ● **Mollie Tower,** Austin Independent School District, Austin, Texas

contents

UNIT 1 AMERICAN MUSIC—SOMETHING FOR EVERYONE!

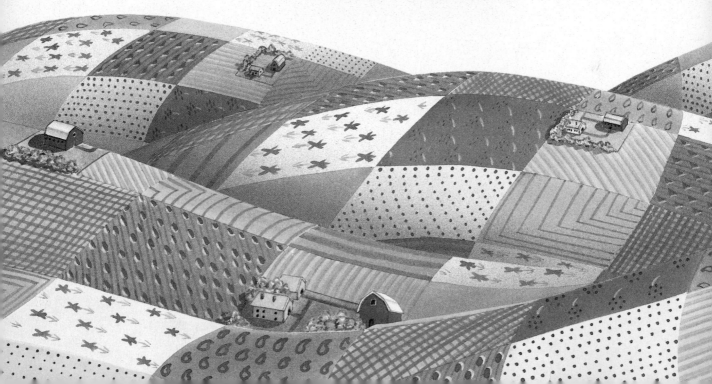

1

BEAT, STRONG BEAT, AND MELODIC RHYTHM

Put yourself in the pictures on page 1. How many ways can you make music?

Keep the beat in different ways as you listen.

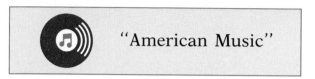 "American Music"

● Clap the strong beat as you listen to the song.

You're a Grand Old Flag

Words and Music by George M. Cohan

You're a grand old flag, you're a high-fly-ing flag;

And for-ev-er in peace may you wave;

You're the em-blem of the land I love,

The home of the free and the brave.

Ev - 'ry heart beats true un - der red, white, and blue,

Where there's nev - er a boast or brag; _____

But should auld ac - quaint - ance be for - got,

Keep your eye on the grand old flag. _____

● Find this **pattern** in the song:

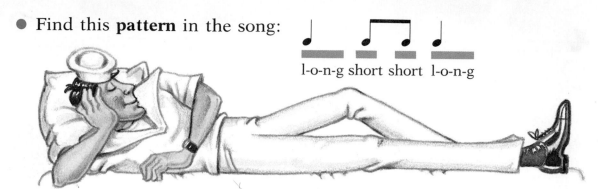

l-o-n-g short short l-o-n-g

Long-Legged Sailor

Game Chant

1. Did you ev - er, ev - er, ev - er in your long - leg - ged life
2. Did you ev - er, ev - er, ev - er in your short - leg - ged life

Meet a   long - leg - ged sail - or with a   long - leg - ged wife?
Meet a   short - leg - ged sail - or with a   short - leg - ged wife?

No I   nev - er, nev - er, nev - er in my   long - leg - ged life,
No I   nev - er, nev - er, nev - er in my   short - leg - ged life,

Met a   long - leg - ged sail - or with a   long - leg - ged wife.
Met a   short - leg - ged sail - or with a   short - leg - ged wife.

3. knock-kneed   4. bow-legged   5. cross-legged

The sign ⌢ over a note means to hold the note
a little longer.

4

UPWARD AND DOWNWARD

Sailors use flags to signal.

How could you signal the upward and downward
direction of the melody?

Which lines in this song end in an upward direction?

Which lines in this song end in a downward direction?

Old Blue

Traditional

1. I had a dog and his name was Blue,
2. Chased that __ pos-sum up a hol - low tree,

I had a dog and his name was Blue.
Chased that __ pos-sum up a hol - low tree.

I had a dog and his name was Blue,
Chased that __ pos-sum up a hol - low tree,

And I bet - cha five dol - lars he's a good dog __ too.
Best __ hunt-in' dog __ you __ ev - er did see.

Here Blue! You good dog, you.
Here Blue! You good dog, you.

3. Caught that possum up a hollow tree, (*three times*)
Best huntin' dog you ever did see.
Here Blue! You good dog, you.

LONG AND SHORT SOUNDS

- Take turns calling Old Blue.
- Use your voice to make high or low and long or short sounds.

H---e---r---e---,

B---l---u---e---

Here,   Here,

Blue   Blue

Oh, Susanna

Words and Music by Stephen Foster

Verse

1. I — come from Al - a - ba - ma With my ban-jo on my knee,
2. I — had a dream the oth-er night, When ev-'ry-thing was still.

I'm – go-ing to Lou-i - si - an - a, My — true love for to see;
I — thought I saw Su - san - na A - com-ing down the hill.

It — rained all night the day I left, The weath-er it was dry;
The – buck-wheat cake was in her mouth, The tear was in her eye.

The – sun so hot I froze to death; Su-san-na, don't you cry.
Says – I, "I'm com-ing from the South, Su-san-na, don't you cry."

Refrain

Oh, Su - san - na, Oh, don't you cry for me,

I — come from Al - a - ba - ma With my ban-jo on my knee.

PITCH STEPS

● Sing your way up and down the pitch steps.

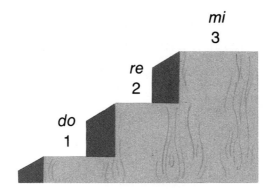

● Find the *do re mi* patterns in "Oh, Susanna."
    1 2 3

TEMPO AND DYNAMICS

Pictures and music can suggest stories.

What is the mood of this picture?

What kind of story might go with this picture of Death Valley?

Tempo and dynamics in music help to show mood.

Tempo means the speed of the beat.

Would the tempo for your story be fast or slow?

Dynamics means levels of soft or loud.

Would the dynamics for your story be loud or soft?

● Listen to this music and tell if this composer used your ideas.

 "Desert Water Hole," from *Death Valley Suite* by Ferde Grofé (fərd′ē grō-fā′)

MUSIC HAS SECTIONS

In 1848 gold was discovered in California. Soon many people began to travel west in covered wagons in hopes of finding gold. The journey was long, hard, and dangerous.

An American composer named Ferde Grofé wrote music to suggest the story of these travelers. This music, called "Desert Water Hole," describes three parts of a day during the journey west.

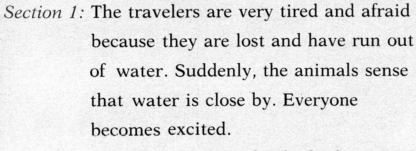

Section 1: The travelers are very tired and afraid because they are lost and have run out of water. Suddenly, the animals sense that water is close by. Everyone becomes excited.

Section 2: The travelers give thanks for having found water.

Section 3: They celebrate by singing and square dancing.

● Listen for the three **sections** in "Desert Water Hole" by Grofé. Differences in tempos and dynamics will help you know when the sections change. What change in tempo would you expect to hear at the end of Section 1?

MORE RHYTHM PATTERNS

● Move to the beat as you listen to "Willowbee." Do one movement during the first (A) section of the song and another during the second (B) section of the song. Do a special movement on the **fermata** 𝄐 .

Willowbee

- Listen to rhythms with more than one sound in a
  beat box.

1	2	3	4

- Point to each beat box to show the rhythm patterns
  you hear.
- Tell which beat has two sounds.

THE UPS AND DOWNS OF MUSIC

When I First Came to This Land

Words and music by Oscar Brand

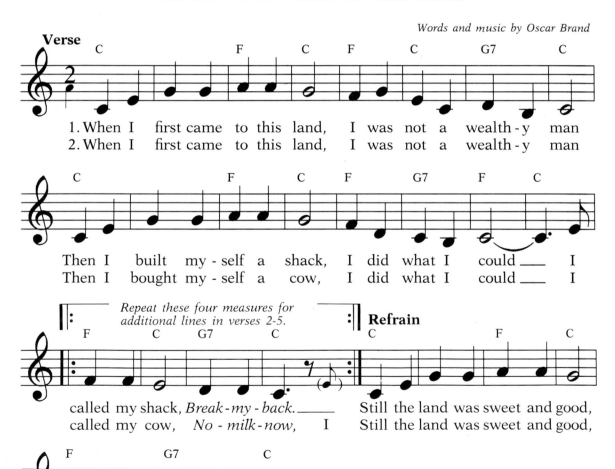

Verse

1. When I first came to this land, I was not a wealth-y man
2. When I first came to this land, I was not a wealth-y man

Then I built my-self a shack, I did what I could ___ I
Then I bought my-self a cow, I did what I could ___ I

Repeat these four measures for additional lines in verses 2-5.

Refrain

called my shack, *Break-my-back.* ___ Still the land was sweet and good,
called my cow, *No-milk-now,* I Still the land was sweet and good,

I did what I could.
I did what I could.

3. When I first came to this land,
   I was not a wealthy man.
   Then I bought myself a horse,
   I did what I could.
   I called my horse, *Lame-of-course,*
   I called my cow, *No-milk-now,*
   I called my shack, *Break-my-back.*
   Still the land was sweet and good,
   I did what I could.

4. When I first came to this land,
   I was not a wealthy man.
   Then I got myself a wife,
   I did what I could.
   I called my wife, *Joy-of-my-life,*
   I called my horse, *Lame-of-course,*
   I called my cow, *No-milk-now,*
   I called my shack, *Break-my-back.*
   Still the land was sweet and good,
   I did what I could.

5. When I first came to this land,
   I was not a wealthy man.
   Then I got myself a son,
   I did what I could.
   I told my son, "My work's done."
   I called my wife, *Joy-of-my-life,*
   I called my horse, *Lame-of-course,*
   I called my cow, *No-milk-now,*
   I called my shack, *Break-my-back.*
   Still the land was sweet and good,
   I did what I could.

"When I First Came to This Land" begins with this pattern.

You know a song that begins like this. What is it?

MUSIC IN TWOS

Music in sets of two can be shown with a **meter signature** of $\frac{2}{2}$ or $\frac{2}{2.}$.

Our Washing Machine

Patricia Hubbell

Our wash - ing ma - chine went whis - i - ty whirr,

Whis - i - ty, whis - i - ty, whis - i - ty whirr.

One day at noon it went whis - i - ty click,

Whis - i - ty, whis - i - ty, whis - i - ty click.

Click grr, click grr, click grr, click.

Call the re - pair - man.

Fix it Quick!

MORE MUSIC IN TWOS

We're Sailing Down the River

Traditional American Tune

Refrain F   B♭   F

We're sail-ing down the riv - er. __ We're sail-ing down be - low. __

F   C7   F   *End (Fine)*

We're sail-ing down the riv - er ___ On the O - hi - o. ___

Verse F

1. Two   in   the   mid - dle   and   you   can't   jump   o - ver!
2. Four   in   the   mid - dle   and   you   can't   jump   o - ver!

F   B♭   C7

Two   in   the   mid - dle   and   you   can't   jump   o - ver!
Four   in   the   mid - dle   and   you   can't   jump   o - ver!

F

Two   in   the   mid - dle   and   you   can't   jump   o - ver!
Four   in   the   mid - dle   and   you   can't   jump   o - ver!

Go back to the beginnning and sing to End. (Da Capo al Fine)

F   C7   F

Oh,   Miss   Su - san   Brown!

3. Hold my mule while I jump over! *(3 times)*
   Oh, Miss Susan Brown! *Refrain*

17

A MUSICAL REVUE

- Perform some of the American music you have learned. You could review the songs in class, sing them for an audience, or tape them.
- Use these songs: "You're a Grand Old Flag," "Long-Legged Sailor," "When I First Came to this Land," "Old Blue," "Our Washing Machine," "We're Sailing Down the River," and "Willowbee."

JUST CHECKING

See how much you remember.

1. Which pattern shows two sounds in each beat?

    a.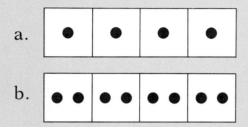

    b.

2. Name the line that has this pattern of long and short sounds:

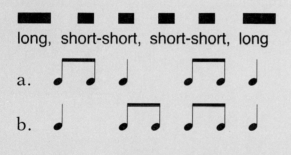

long, short-short, short-short, long

    a.

    b.

3. Does ♩ ♫ ♫ ♩ | go with the words *pease porridge in the pot?*

4. Which is the highest pitch in this example?

    Does this melody move upward or downward?

5. Which song begins with this pattern?

19

UNIT 2 FUN IN AUTUMN

TEMPO

● Imagine a garden in the autumn as
you listen to this poem.

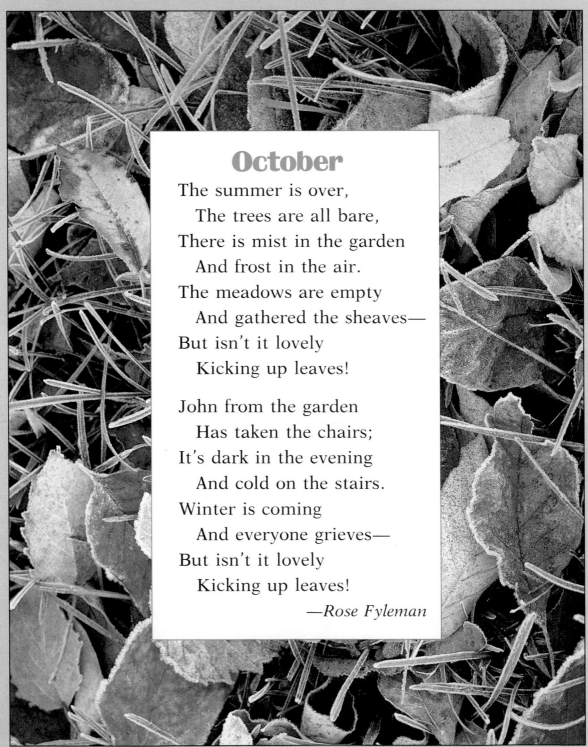

October

The summer is over,
　The trees are all bare,
There is mist in the garden
　And frost in the air.
The meadows are empty
　And gathered the sheaves—
But isn't it lovely
　Kicking up leaves!

John from the garden
　Has taken the chairs;
It's dark in the evening
　And cold on the stairs.
Winter is coming
　And everyone grieves—
But isn't it lovely
　Kicking up leaves!

—Rose Fyleman

In music tempo means the speed of the beat.

● Listen for tempo changes in this music.

 "Voiles" from *Preludes, Book 1,* by Claude Debussy (klôd deb-yoo-sē')

● Listen again and move to show the tempo changes.

The artist, Claude Monet, painted many outdoor scenes. This picture, *On the Cliffs,* is one of Monet's paintings. Monet spent many hours studying the way sunlight changes the way things look. He often painted the same scene at different times of the day. To show light on this scene Monet used very pale colors. Both the artist Monet and the composer Debussy lived in France. They lived and worked at about the same time.

Li'l 'Liza Jane

American Dance-Game Song

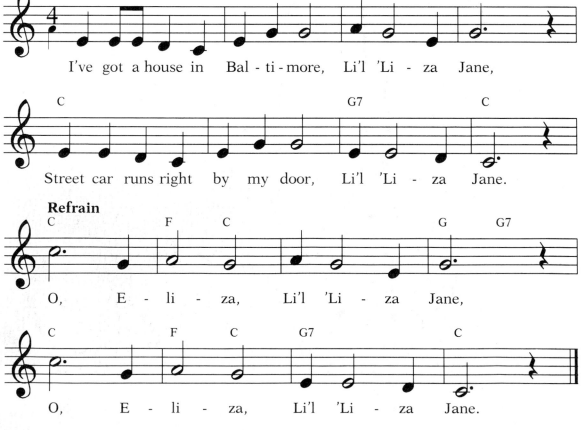

I've got a house in Bal - ti - more, Li'l 'Li - za Jane,

Street car runs right by my door, Li'l 'Li - za Jane.

Refrain

O, E - li - za, Li'l 'Li - za Jane,

O, E - li - za, Li'l 'Li - za Jane.

HIGH AND LOW PITCHES

● Find the highest pitch in "Li'l 'Liza Jane."

Here is one way people make music together.

● Think of other ways people make music together.

- Find the highest pitch in this song. It is called *la* or 6.
- Find the next pitch lower than *la*. It is called *so* or 5.

Rocky Mountain

Southern Folk Song

Rock-y Moun-tain, Rock-y Moun-tain, Rock-y Moun-tain high,

When you're on that Rock-y Moun-tain, hang your head and cry.

Do, do, do, do, Do re-mem-ber me.

Do, do, do, do, Do re-mem-ber me.

● Make up your own melodies.

Here are all the pitches in the song "Rocky Mountain."

The bells for these pitches are pictured below.

● Take turns making up melodies using these pitches.
● Play melodies that sound like going up and down
  a mountain.

Sometimes music is used to suggest a story.

● Listen to music that tells a funny story about a lazy
boy. Listen for the very high and very low sounds.

 The Sorcerer's Apprentice, by **Paul Dukas** (dōō-ka′)

● After you listen to the music and know the story, act
it out.

NOTES—SHORT, LONG, AND LONGER

Are You Sleeping?

(Frère Jacques)

French Folk Song

1 F

Are you sleep - ing, are you sleep - ing,
Frè - re Jac - ques, Frè - re Jac - ques,

2 F

Broth - er John, Broth - er John?
Dor - mez - vous, dor - mez - vous?

F

Morn - ing bells are ring - ing, morn - ing bells are ring - ing,
Son - nez les ma - ti - nes, son - nez les ma - ti - nes,

F

Ding, ding, dong, ding, ding, dong.
Din, din, don, din, din, don.

A **quarter note** ♩ sounds for one beat in this song.

● Play quarter notes on rhythm sticks to make the
sound of a ticking clock.

A **half note** ♩ sounds for two beats in "Are You Sleeping?"

- Find the half notes in the song.
- Play this pattern of half notes on an instrument while you sing the song. On which beats will you play?

Beats: 1 2 3 4

- Do a pat-clap-clap pattern as you sing this song.
- Make the sounds shown below each time you see * in the refrain.

The Alpine Song

Traditional
(Austrian Yodelling Song)
Words adapted by Susan Van Dyck

1. Oh, an Aus-tri-an went yo-del-ling on a moun-tain so high.
2. Oh, an Aus-tri-an went yo-del-ling on a moun-tain so high.

When a-long came an a-va-lanche in-ter-rupt-ing his cry.
When a-long came a Saint Ber-nard in-ter-rupt-ing his cry.

Refrain

Yo-lay-dee, yo-de-lay-hee-hoo, Oh yo-de-lay-hee-hoo.

Yo-de-lay-hee-hoo, Oh yo-de-lay-hee-hoo. Yo-de-lay-hee-hoo,

Oh, yo-de-lay-hee-hoo. Yo-de-lay-hee-hoo-oh lay.

1. * shhh-shhh . . .
2. * pant-pant, shhh-shhh . . .
3. . . . When along came a Guernsey Cow . . .
   * moo-moo, pant-pant, shhh-shhh . . .
4. . . . When along came a Martian . . .
   * beep-beep, moo-moo, pant-pant, shhh-shhh . . .

What does 🎵 mean?

● Play **dotted half notes** (𝅗𝅥.) on the verses of "The Alpine Song." Start playing on the first beat of the measure and let the sound continue on the second and third beats. A dotted half note sounds for three beats in this song. Count the beats in your head, "One, two, three."

$\frac{3}{\text{♩}}$ ‖: 𝅗𝅥. | 𝅗𝅥. | 𝅗𝅥. | 𝅗𝅥. :‖

PLAYING THE AUTOHARP

The instrument in this photograph is an **Autoharp.**

You can play **chords** with an Autoharp.

Chords are three or more pitches sounding together.

- Practice pressing the chord buttons on an Autoharp with your left hand.
- Bring your right hand over your left hand and strum the strings. Begin with the strings nearest to you and strum away from yourself.

- Find the chord symbols in songs that you know. They are above each **staff**.

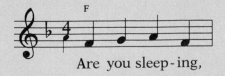

Are you sleep-ing,

- Play the chords on the strong beats for "Are You Sleeping?" and "The Alpine Song."

MYSTERIOUS TONE COLORS

Tone colors are the special sounds made by each instrument or voice.

● Make these words sound mysterious by changing the tone color of your voice. Say them in different ways.

● Listen for changes in instrumental tone color in this music about an Irish spirit called a banshee.

The Banshee, by Henry Cowell

All the sounds you heard were made on one instrument.

What instrument do you think was being played?

How were the different sounds made?

What instrument could you use to make sounds like these?

● Use different tone colors with "Skin and Bones."

Choose a different instrument sound to play at the end
of each verse. Play it when you see this sign: ♩

Add an Autoharp accompaniment.

Sing the song with spooky tone color and act it out.

Skin and Bones

Folk Song from Kentucky
Collected by Jean Ritchie

1. There was an old wom-an all skin and bones, Oo-oo-oo-ooh!
2. She lived down by the old grave-yard, Oo-oo-oo-ooh!

3. One night she thought she'd take a walk, Oo-oo-oo-ooh!

4. She walked down by the old graveyard, Oo-oo-oo-ooh!

5. She saw the bones a-layin' around, Oo-oo-oo-ooh!

6. She went to the closet to get a broom, Oo-oo-oo-ooh!

7. She opened the door and **BOO!!**

- Play a classroom instrument in a new way to make a different sound.
- Add some of your sounds to this poem.

Hallowe'en

Tonight is the night
When dead leaves fly
Like witches on switches
Across the sky,
When elf and sprite
Flit through the night
On a moony sheen.

Tonight is the night
When leaves make a sound
Like a gnome in his home
Under the ground,
When spooks and trolls
Creep out of holes
Mossy and green.

Tonight is the night
When pumpkins stare
Through sheaves and leaves
Everywhere,
When ghoul and ghost
And goblin host
Dance round their queen.
It's Hallowe'en!

—*Harry Behn*

From THE LITTLE HILL, Poems & Pictures by Harry Behn. Copyright 1949 by Harry Behn, © renewed 1977 by Alice L Behn. Used by permission of Marian Reiner.

LOUD AND SOFT

Which section is loud?

Which section is soft?

Halloween Night

Words and Music by
Doris Parker

1. Bet - ter watch out it's Hal - lo - ween night.
2. Bet - ter watch out it's Hal - lo - ween night.

Look at all the spoo - ky sights. __
Look at all the spoo - ky sights. __

Bet - ter watch out it's Hal - lo - ween night.
Bet - ter watch out it's Hal - lo - ween night.

Look at all the spoo - ky sights. __
Look at all the spoo - ky sights. __

Skel - e - tons, let's have some fun.
Witch - es, too, what can you do?

When I count to eight you must be done. __
When I count to eight you must be through. __

One   two   three   four   five   six   seven   eight.

3. Better watch out it's Halloween night.
   Look at all the spooky sights.
   Better watch out it's Halloween night.
   Look at all the spooky sights.
   Goblins and ghosts, how can you fly?
   When I count to eight, come down from the sky.

- Look for *p* and *f* in "Halloween Night."

  p stands for **piano,** which means soft.

  f stands for **forte,** which means loud.

- Practice saying the words *piano* and *forte.*

- Watch for these signs as you sing "Halloween Night" and other music. Be sure to sing or play softly when you see *p* and use more energy when you see *f*

REMEMBERING FUN IN AUTUMN

- Act out some fast things and some slow things that you do during autumn. The picture below can give you some ideas.

- Look at pages 22–41 and choose favorite songs or poems.

- Sing a song or say a poem in two different tempos.

- Perform a song or poem from this unit using different tone colors made by instruments or your voice.

- Sing a song and show the high and low pitches with hand movements.

JUST CHECKING

See how much you remember.

1. Which is the lower note in each example?

2. What are the syllables or scale numbers of the pitches on the staff below? The first one is named for you.

do
1

3. The bells for these pitches are pictured below.

Are the bells in order from lowest to highest?

UNIT 3

STRINGED INSTRUMENTS IN FOLK MUSIC

STRINGS IN FOLK MUSIC

Each country has its own folk music. In the United States, the stringed instruments often used to accompany folk songs are the banjo, guitar, and Appalachian dulcimer. In the past, as today, folk instruments were made by hand out of materials found nearby. These instruments are played by either picking or strumming the strings.

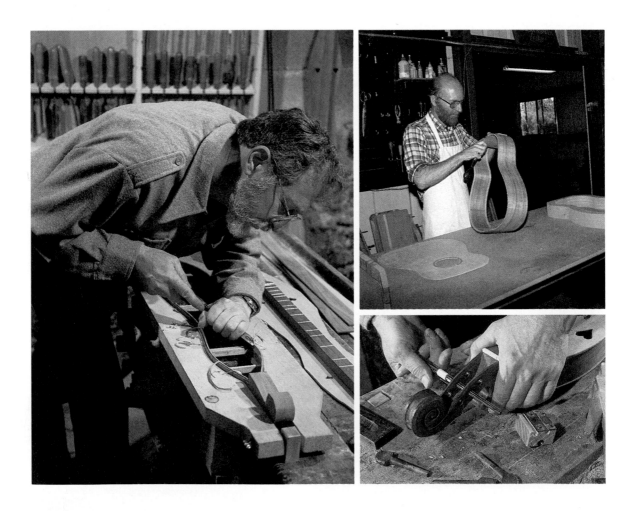

These skilled workers are making a dulcimer and a guitar. Favorite woods used often include walnut, spruce, and curly maple.

The **banjo** is often played in folk music. It has a metal or wooden body with a tightly stretched skin on the top. The neck of the banjo is very long and thin. On most banjos the neck is divided into sections by thin metal bars called **frets.** When the player's fingers move to different frets, the pitch becomes higher or lower.

Banjos can also be hand crafted like guitars and dulcimers, and have either four or five strings.

What stringed instrument do you hear?

My Home's in Montana

Cowboy Song

1. My home's in Mon - tan - a, I wear a ban - dan - na;
2. When val - leys are dust - y, My po - ny is trust - y;

My spurs are of sil - ver, My po - ny is gray.
He lopes through the bliz - zard, The snow in his ears.

When rid - ing the rang - es My luck nev - er chang - es:
The cat - tle may scat - ter, But what does it mat - ter!

With foot in the stir - rup I'll gal - lop a - way.
My rope is a hal - ter For pig - head - ed steers.

3. When far from the ranches,
   I chop the pine branches
   To heap on my campfire
   As daylight grows pale;
   When I have partaken
   Of beans and of bacon,
   I whistle a merry
   Old song of the trail.

● Pretend to play a guitar.

Use your right hand:

strum strum strum

The **guitar** is played in many types of music: folk, classical, jazz, and rock. The folk guitar is made of wood and usually has six strings. The neck of the guitar also has frets.

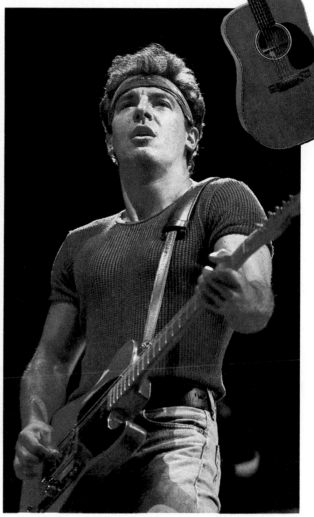

● Listen to "Dueling Banjos." What instruments do you hear?

 "Dueling Banjos", by Eric Weisberg

Why do you think this piece is called "Dueling Banjos?"

STRONG BEAT AND METER

● Point to a stick in the drawing below for every beat as you listen to "Indian Stick Song." Start the line again when you run out of sticks.

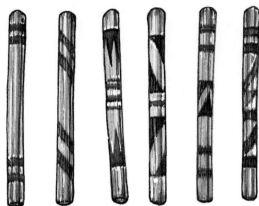

Beats can also be shown by quarter notes. Here is another way of showing the same sound.

● Point to the quarter notes as you listen again for the strong beats. Press a little harder when you hear them.

The beats are grouped in sets of three. The number of beats in each set is the **meter.**

The meter sign is $\frac{3}{4}$

This is a totem pole made of carved and painted wood. Its symbols represent ancestors, history, and stories of a northwestern Indian tribe.

● Find the strong beat in this song.

Indian Stick Song

Northwest Coast Native American Game

Ma koo - ay Ko tay - o Ay - koo-ee tah - nah.

Ma koo - ay Ko tay - o Ay - koo-ee tah - nah.

● Use rhythm sticks to play this stick game.

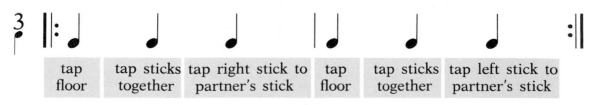

| tap floor | tap sticks together | tap right stick to partner's stick | tap floor | tap sticks together | tap left stick to partner's stick |

● Create a part for a rattle using ♩.

In ¾ ♩. sounds as long as ♩ ♩ ♩

51

- Tap a pattern to show how beats are grouped into sets in this song.
- Decide if the song has a meter of two or three.
- Find the meter sign in the song.

Who Did?

African American Spiritual

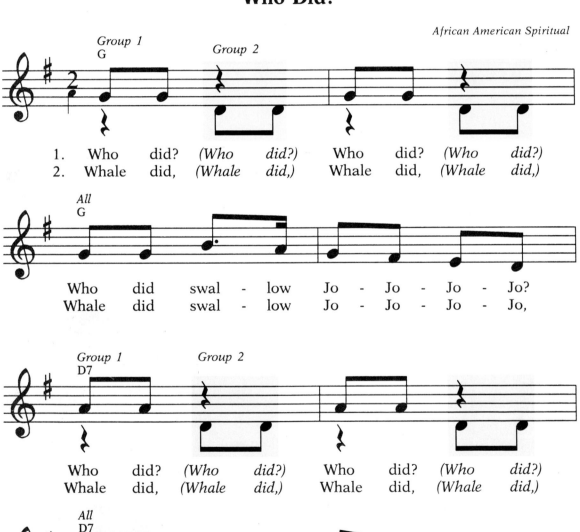

Group 1
G

Group 2

1. Who did? (Who did?) Who did? (Who did?)
2. Whale did, (Whale did,) Whale did, (Whale did,)

All
G

Who did swal - low Jo - Jo - Jo - Jo?
Whale did swal - low Jo - Jo - Jo - Jo,

Group 1
D7

Group 2

Who did? (Who did?) Who did? (Who did?)
Whale did, (Whale did,) Whale did, (Whale did,)

All
D7

Who did swal - low Jo - Jo - Jo - Jo?
Whale did swal - low Jo - Jo - Jo - Jo,

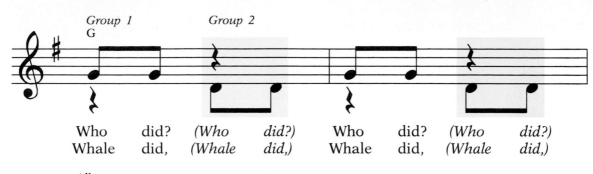

Who did? *(Who did?)* Who did? *(Who did?)*
Whale did, *(Whale did,)* Whale did, *(Whale did,)*

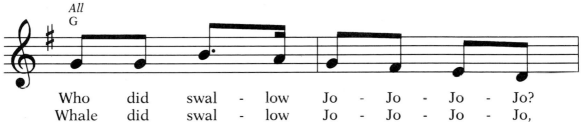

Who did swal - low Jo - Jo - Jo - Jo?
Whale did swal - low Jo - Jo - Jo - Jo,

Who did swal - low Jo - nah? *(Who did swal - low*
Whale did swal - low Jo - nah, *(Whale did swal - low*

Jo - nah?) Who did swal - low Jo - nah down? ____
Jo - nah,) Whale did swal - low Jo - nah up. _____

3. Daniel, *(Daniel,)* Daniel, *(Daniel,)*
   Daniel in the li-li-li-li, *(3 times)*
   Daniel in the lion's, *(Daniel in the lion's,)*
   Daniel in the lion's den.

4. Gabriel, *(Gabriel,)* Gabriel, *(Gabriel,)*
   Gabriel blow your trump-trump-trump-trump, *(3 times)*
   Gabriel blow your trumpet, *(Gabriel blow your trumpet,)*
   Gabriel blow your trumpet loud.

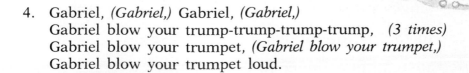

● Listen to "John Henry."

 "John Henry," Traditional American Ballad

You can hear the **Appalachian dulcimer** in "John Henry." It is a stringed instrument used in American folk music. It comes from the Appalachian mountains of the eastern United States. It is made of wood like the guitar and banjo, but has a different shape.

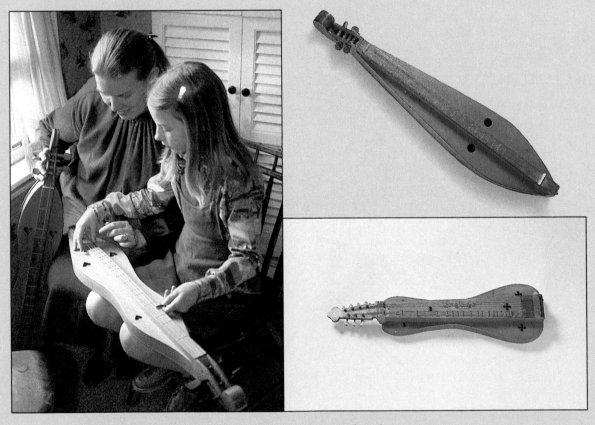

The Appalachian dulcimer is played on the lap or on a table. The player strums the strings with the right hand. The left hand index finger presses and slides on the first string to create a melody. In the picture above a noter, or small round stick, is used instead of a finger to play the melody.

54

METER: LISTEN AND LOOK

What is the meter of this song?

Hop-a-Doodle

American Folk Song

Down in the mead - ow, Hop - a - dood - le, Hop - a - dood - le.

Down in the mead - ow Hop - a - dood - le doo.

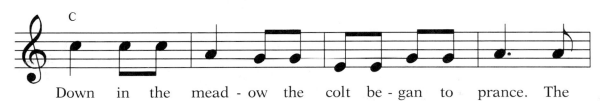

Down in the mead - ow the colt be - gan to prance. The

cow be - gan to whis - tle, and the pig be - gan to dance.

This dulcimer, called the **hammered dulcimer,** is played
with "Hop-a-Doodle." Its strings are struck with beaters.

PLAYING BELLS

- Use the pictures below to help you find the right bells to play.

- Play this bell part with "My Home's in Montana."

My Home's in Montana

- Play this bell part with "Who Did?"

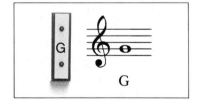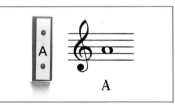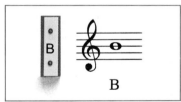

Who Did?

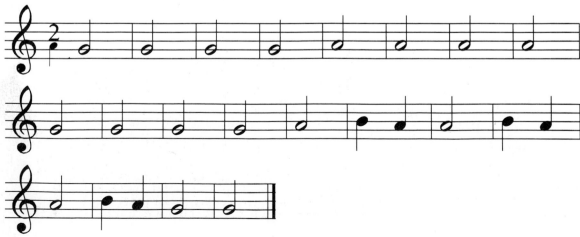

INSTRUMENTAL TONE COLOR

- Find the G and D7 chord buttons on the Autoharp.
- Practice strumming these chords as you sing "Who Did?"

G
Who did? (Who did?)

G
Who did swallow

D7
Who did? (Who did?)

D7
Who did swallow

G
Who did? (Who did?)

G
Who did swallow

D7   D7
Who did swallow Jonah?

D7   D7
Who did swallow Jonah

G
Who did? (Who did?)

G
Jo - Jo - Jo - Jo?

D7
Who did? (Who did?)

D7
Jo - Jo - Jo - Jo?

G
Who did? (Who did?)

G
Jo - Jo - Jo - Jo?

D7   D7
(Who did swallow Jonah?)

G
down?

● Listen to "Thanksgiving."

What instrument plays the
melody in this song?

Thanksgiving

Words and Music by Constance Heidt

Thanks-giv-ing,   Thanks-giv-ing,   Thanks-

giv-ing is the time of year when peo-ple think a - bout   their

fam-'ly   to - geth-er,   think-ing of the

things that   peo - ple   ought to   think   a - bout.

Good-ness,   kind-ness,   shar-ing,   Thanks-giv-ing.

Thanks-giv-ing,   Thanks-giv-ing,   Thanks-

giv-ing is the time of year when peo-ple think a-bout good-ness,

kind-ness, shar-ing to-geth-er for ev-er.

What familiar melody do you recognize in this song?

On Thanksgiving

Traditional Melody
Words by M.S. and B.S.

1. On Thanks-giv-ing, on Thanks-giv-ing,
2. On Thanks-giv-ing, on Thanks-giv-ing,

Come to dine, be on time.
Foot-ball game, glad we came.

First we have a greet-ing, then we start the eat-ing;
Af-ter tur-key din-ner, we will know the win-ner;

Eat all day, that's the way.
If we lose, take a snooze.

- Play a different instrument on each set of rhyming words.

- Name some things for which you are thankful.

The First Thanksgiving

When the Pilgrims
first gathered together to share
with their Indian friends
in the mild autumn air,
they lifted their voices
in jubilant praise
for the bread on the table,
the berries and maize,
for field and for forest,
for turkey and deer,
for the bountiful crops
they were blessed with that year.
They were thankful for these
as they feasted away,
and as they were thankful,
we're thankful today.

—*Jack Prelutsky*

The First Thanksgiving at Plymouth, Jennie A. Brownscombe

PARTS OF SONGS

An **introduction** is music that comes before a song.

An **interlude** is music that is in between the main parts
of a song.

A **coda** is music that is at the end of a song.

● Play this on the bells as an
introduction and coda for
this song.

B   A   A   G

● Make up an interlude using the pitches B A and G.

Lullaby

*Words and Music by
Carole King*

All thru the night,   the moon is sil-ver bright.   Crick-et sings his

ti-ny song, sings it thru the whole night long. All thru the night.

LISTEN AND REMEMBER

You have heard the sounds of the stringed instruments pictured here. They are used to accompany many of the American folk songs that you learned.

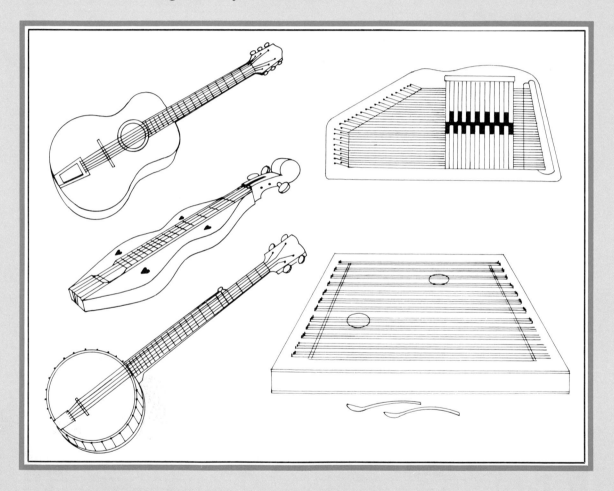

- Listen again and do a pat, clap, clap pattern when the music is in sets of three.
- Name the instruments. Point to each instrument as you hear it in "Sounds of Folk Stringed Instruments."
- Tell which song is in $\frac{3}{4}$ meter.

JUST CHECKING

See how much you remember.

1. Point to the word below which means the speed of the beat.

   time   dulcimer   tempo   staff

2. Name the three instruments shown here:

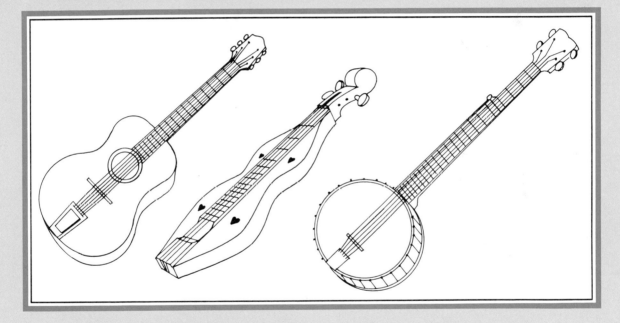

3. Point to the note below that lasts as long as three quarter notes ♩ ♩ ♩

   a. ♩   b. ♩.   c. 𝅝

4. Which note lasts as long as two quarter notes?

   a. ♩   b. ♩.   c. 𝅝

UNIT 4

SOUNDS OF THE HOLIDAY SEASON

A Very Happy Christmas

TONE COLOR FOR SPECIAL DAYS

● Listen for sounds of the holiday season.

"Happy Holidays!"

- Listen to the music for the words *happy holidays*.
- Play an echo to the words *happy holidays* using the G and A bells. Start on G.

In which section do you hear the banjo?

Christmas Is Joy

*Words and music by
David and Phyllis Stycos*

Christ-mas is joy ___ when ev-'ry-one's hap - py. ___
Christ-mas is giv - ing one to an - oth - er. ___

Christ-mas is love ___ when ev-'ry-one cares! ___
Hal - le - lu - ia! ___ There's joy in the air! ___

Joy ___ Joy ___ Come join us in bro - ther-hood.

Joy ___ Joy ___ Now ev-'ry-one's feel - in' good!

Joy ___ Joy ___ Let's cel - e-brate as ___ we may.

Go back to the beginning and sing to the End.
(Da Capo al Fine)

Joy ___ Joy ___ Come sing it this hap - py day!

68

- Say the letter name of each pitch as you point to the bell with the same name. Then sing the letters.

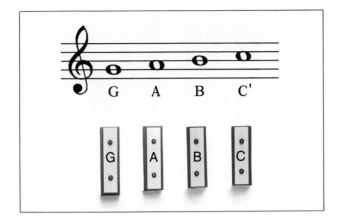

How many different bells will you use to play this bell part?

- Play these bells only on the strong beat except in the next to the last measure.

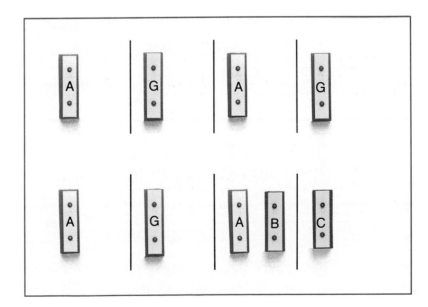

- Play the bell part during the A section of "Christmas Is Joy."

● Play the tambourine two different ways as you sing
   this song. A different tone color is created when an
   instrument is played in a different way.

Hanukah

Hebrew Folk Song

Ha - nu - kah,   Ha - nu - kah,   Mer - ry hol - i - day!

Ha - nu - kah,   Ha - nu - kah,   Time to dance and   play.

Ha - nu - kah,   Ha - nu - kah,   Bright the can - dles burn.

Round and round, round and round, Watch the drey - dl turn.

The dreydl is a favorite Hanukah toy. One of the sounds of the holiday season is the sound of the spinning of this four-sided top. On each side of the dreydl is a different Hebrew letter. These letters stand for the words *Ness godol hayah sham,* which means "A great miracle happened here."

The menorah is a candle holder used during Hanukah.

One candle is lit for each of the eight nights of Hanukah.

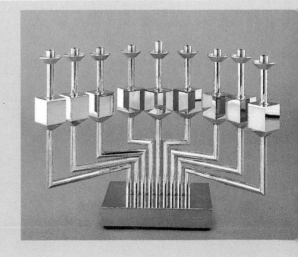

FINDING METER

● Pat the strong beat as you listen to this song.

Andale Juana

Mexican Folk Song

Verse

Ⓐ

C   F   C

¡An - da - le   Jua - na,   no   te   di - la - tes;
Hur - ry   up   Jua - na,   do   not   de - lay   now;

C   G7   C

Trae   la   cha - ro - la   de   los   ca - ca - hue - tes!
Bring   out   the   bas - ket   of   chest - nuts   and   pea - nuts!

C   F   C

No   quie - ro   pla - ta,   no   quie - ro   o - ro;
I   don't   want   sil - ver,   I   don't   want   gold; —

C   G7   C

yo   lo   que   quie - ro es rom - per   la   pi - ña - ta.
all   that   I   want   is   to   break   the   pi - ña - ta.

Refrain

Ⓑ

C   F   C

La   la   la   la   la   la   la   la   La   la   la

G7   C

la   la   la   La   la   la   la   la   la   La

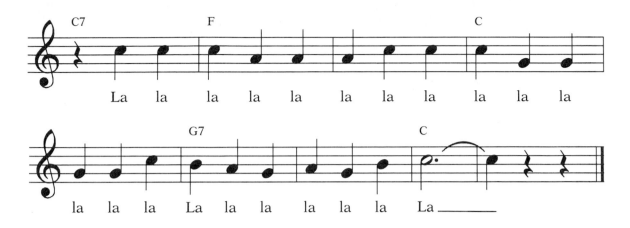

La la la la la la la la la la la

la la la La la la la la la La____

How many beats are in each measure?

Which is the strong beat?

A **mariachi** is a Mexican street band. Musicians in a
mariachi wear colorful costumes as they sing and play
their instruments. Mariachi music uses the instruments
shown on this page.

guitarrón   vihuela

What instruments can you name?

These instruments are heard with "Andale Juana."

In Mexican and Mexican-American homes, families take part in a ceremony called Las Posadas. This ceremony is based on the story of Mary and Joseph searching for an inn in Bethlehem long ago. A group of families or friends walk to someone's home to ask for a place to stay. At first they are refused but finally they are allowed to enter. They do this on each of the nine nights before Christmas. "Andale Juana" and "Dale, Dale, Dale!" are songs that are sung during Las Posadas.

The people feast and celebrate after each Posada ceremony. The children play a game with a piñata. A piñata is a large hollow bird or animal made of clay or papier-mâché. It is filled with nuts, fruits, sweets, and small presents and hangs from the ceiling or a pole. Children take turns trying to break the piñata with a stick. Soon everything spills onto the floor. Then everyone scrambles to collect the treats.

This is a song about breaking the piñata.

● Listen for the sound of the Mariachi. Pat the strong beat.

Dale (dä'le) means "hit it."

74

Dale, Dale, Dale!

Mexican Folk Song

Verse

En las no-ches de po-sa - das, la pi - ña-ta es lo me - jor, _____
On the nights of Las Po - sa - das, chil-dren laugh and try with all their might,

Y los ni-ños mas a - le - gres le pe-gan con gran fer-vor. _
For to win the bright pi - ña-ta's trea-sure they swing and swing all night. _

Refrain

Da - le, da - le, da - le, no pier-das el ti - no,
Da - le, da - le, da - le, do not lose "el ti - no,"

mi - de la dis - tan - cia, que hay en el ca - mi - no.
Turn a - round and find it on _____ "el ca - mi - no."

Que si no - le das de un pa - lo - te pi - no,
For if you should miss it with "pa - lo - te pi - no,"

por - que tie - nes au - ra, de pu - ro pe - pi - no. _____
you will feel as fool - ish as "pu - ro pe - pi - no." _____

Is the pattern of strong and weak beats the same in both

the A section and B section?

75

Music in $\frac{2}{4}$ meter moves in twos. The first beat is the strong beat and the second beat is weaker.

● Try showing meter in two this way:

Clap wrists on strong beats.   Tap fingers on weak beats.

Think of songs you know that move in twos.

Music in $\frac{3}{4}$ meter moves in threes.
The first beat is the strong beat. The second and third beats are weaker.

● Try showing meter in three in this way:

Think of songs you know that move in threes.

Which hand pattern fits this song?

What is the meter?

Hanukah Time

Jewish Folk Tune

Drey - dl, drey - dl, drey - dl, turn, turn, turn,

Can - dles, can - dles, can - dles, burn, burn, burn,

Shine so bright - ly as we cel - e - brate,

Now as Ha - nu - kah we cel - e - brate.

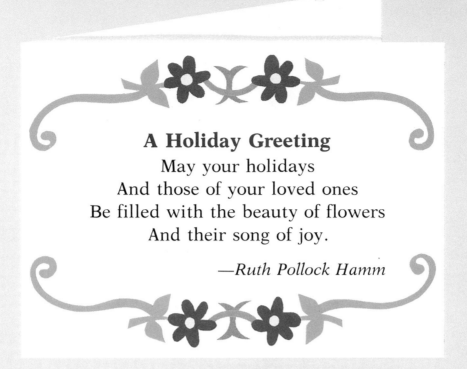

A Holiday Greeting
May your holidays
And those of your loved ones
Be filled with the beauty of flowers
And their song of joy.

—*Ruth Pollock Hamm*

● Pretend to walk through the garden as you listen to "Waltz of the Flowers." Point to a different object for each musical idea. Tap the strong beat on the flowers.

 "Waltz of the Flowers" from *The Nutcracker,* by Peter Ilyich Tchaikovsky (chī kof' skē)

Introduction

Coda

READING RHYTHMS

- Imagine a toy like the one in this song!

- Find this pattern in the refrain.

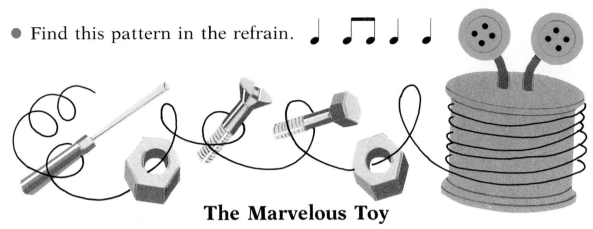

The Marvelous Toy

Words and music by Tom Paxton

1. When I was just a wee lit-tle lad, full of health and joy,
2. The first time that I picked it ___ up I had a big sur-prise,

my fa - ther home - ward came one night, __ and gave to me a toy.
for right on its bottom were two big buttons that looked like big green eyes,

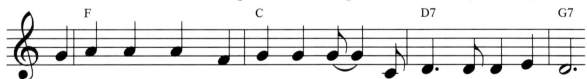

A won - der to be - hold it was, with man - y col - ors bright,
I first pushed one and then the other, And then I twisted its lid,

and the mo - ment I laid eyes on it, it be - came my heart's de - light.
And ___ when I set it down a - gain, ___ Here is what it did:

Refrain

It went zip when it moved and bop when it stopped and whirr when it stood still,

I nev-er knew just what it was and I guess I nev-er will.

3. It first marched left and then marched right and then marched under a chair,
And when I looked where it had gone, it wasn't even there!
I started to sob and my daddy laughed, for he knew that I would find,
When I turned around, my marvelous toy, chugging from behind. *Refrain*

4. Well, the years have gone by too quickly, it seems,
and I have my own little boy,
And yesterday I gave to him my marvelous little toy.
His eyes nearly popped right out of his head and he gave a squeal of glee,
Neither one of us knows just what it is, but he loves it, just like me.

It still goes zip when it moves and bop when it stops,
and whirr when it stands still,
I never knew just what it was,
And I guess I never will.

Twittering Machine. 1922, Paul Klee. Watercolor, pen and ink. 16¼ x 12" (without margins). Purchase. Collection THE MUSEUM OF MODERN ART N.Y.

Paul Klee used simple lines to create a piece of modern art.

● Imagine how this Twittering Machine would move.

"The Twittering Machine" by Gunther Schuller from *Seven Studies on Themes of Paul Klee*

VOCAL TONE COLOR

● As you sing this song, listen to the sound of your voice
and the voices around you.

Pat-a-Pan

Early Burgundian French Carol
Words adapted by M.S.

1. Wil - lie take your lit - tle drum, Rob - in bring your flute and
2. When the lit - tle child was born long a - go that Christ - mas

come. Play a joy - ous tune to - day. *Tu - re - lu - re - lu, pat - a - pat - a -*
morn, Shep - herds came from fields a - far, *Tu - re - lu - re - lu, pat - a - pat - a -*

pan, Play a joy - ous tune to - day on this joy - ous hol - i - day.
pan, Shep - herds came from fields a - far guid - ed by the shin - ing star.

3. Now we celebrate this day on our instruments we play.
Let our voices loudly ring,
Tu-re-lu-re-lu, pat-a-pat-a-pan,
Let our voices loudly ring, as our song and gifts we bring.

● Listen to this song as it is performed by an
elementary school chorus.

 "Pat-a-Pan" performed by the Chevy Chase
Elementary School Chorus, Chevy Chase, Maryland.

How is the chorus performance different from the way
your class sang "Pat-a-Pan"?

PITCH NAMES

Other countries have December celebrations, too.
Kwanzaa is a holiday based on an African
harvest celebration that comes late in December.
It is a Swahili word meaning "first" and stands for the
first fruits of the harvest.

The kinara, a candle holder that holds seven candles, is
an important symbol of Kwanzaa. Beginning
December 26, families light one candle for each of the
seven nights of the celebration.
People celebrate the last evening of Kwanzaa with
music, dancing, gifts, and special food. It is a time for
friends to gather and give thanks for their blessings.

This song might be sung any time of year in Nigeria.

● Pretend to paddle a boat as you sing it.

Nigerian Boat Song

Traditional African Song

Eh Soom boo ka - wa - ya ke - doom ka - dee

Eh Soom boo ka - wa - ya ke - doom ka - dee

ke - doom ka - dee ke - doom ka - dee

ah _____

Soom boo ka - wa - ya kee - doom ka - dee

● Play the pitches in the fourth line on resonator bells.

What are their names?

FAMILIAR TEMPOS AND PITCHES

● Play these bells.

G   A   B

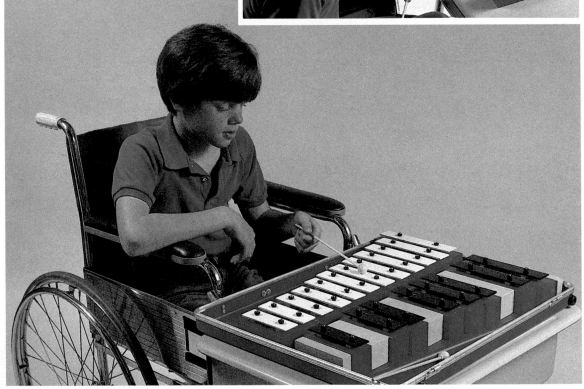

This song is a lullaby.

Do you think this song should be sung at a slow or fast tempo?

● Look carefully at the music as you listen to it. In what way are all the measures alike?

● Name the pitches in the song.

Suo Gan
(sē-ō gahn)

Traditional Welsh Folk Melody

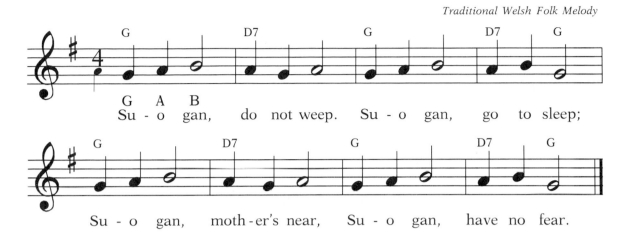

Su - o gan, do not weep. Su - o gan, go to sleep;

Su - o gan, moth-er's near, Su - o gan, have no fear.

Why should this song be sung softly?

How has the artist suggested a quiet mood

in this picture?

SOUNDS OF SPECIAL DAYS
NEAR AND FAR

● Sing favorite holiday songs that might be heard at this time of the year around the world.

● Play the bell parts.

"Happy Holidays" page 66
"Christmas Is Joy," page 68

"Andale Juana," page 72

"Dale, Dale, Dale!" page 75

"Nigerian Boat Song," page 85

"Hanukah," page 70
"Hanukah Time," page 77

JUST CHECKING

See how much you remember.

1. Which beat is the strong beat in $\frac{3}{\text{♩}}$ meter?

    a. second

    b. first

    c. third

2. Give the correct letter name of each pitch.

 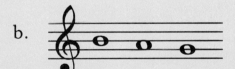

3. What combination of words describes the pattern of beats in $\frac{2}{\text{♩}}$ meter?

    a. strong   weak

    b. weak   strong

    c. strong   strong

UNIT 5

THE MANY SOUNDS OF STRINGS

INSTRUMENT GROUPS

All Who Born in January

Folk Song from Trinidad

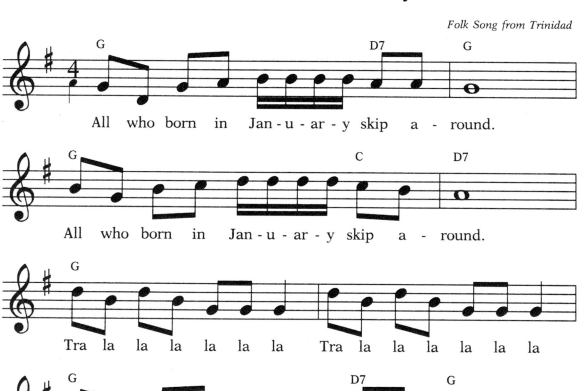

All who born in Jan - u - ar - y skip a - round.

All who born in Jan - u - ar - y skip a - round.

Tra la la la la la la Tra la la la la la la

All who born in Jan - u - ar - y skip a - round.

What other month name has the same rhythm as the
word *Jan-u-ar-y?*

What group of instruments do you hear in "All Who
Born in January"?

Folk Strings

banjo

Appalachian
dulcimer

guitar

In the photographs you
see two groups of
stringed instruments.

Bowed Orchestral Strings

cello

string
bass

viola

violin

● Listen for the sound of the violin, cello, and string bass.

 "Bowed Orchestral Strings"

Detail from *Concert*, Pieter Codde, PUSHKIN MUSEUM, Moscow

● Listen to "Gigue" and pretend to play the violin.

A **gigue** is a dance.

Move your bow to show what happens to the tempo at the end.

The music term that describes this is ***ritard.***

 "Gigue" from *The Suite for Strings,* by Arcangelo Corelli

What strings do you hear in this song?

Welcome, Friends

Words and music by John Horman

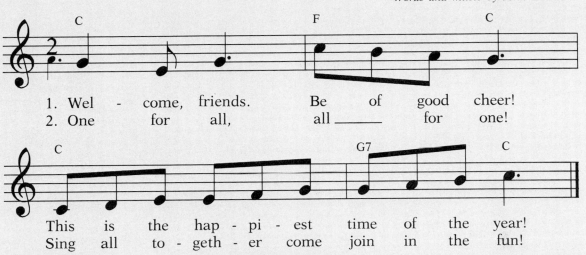

1. Wel - come, friends.   Be of good cheer!
2. One for all,   all _____ for one!

This is the hap - pi - est time of the year!
Sing all to - geth - er come join in the fun!

A NEW PITCH (HIGH *do*)

- Point to the pitches you already know.
- Find the new pitch.

High *do* is the same as *do*' or 8 or 1'.

● Raise your hand when you hear *do'*.

Sarasponda

Dutch Spinning Song

Sa - ra - spon - da, Sa - ra - spon - da, Sa - ra - spon - da, Ret - set - set!

Sa - ra - spon - da, Sa - ra - spon - da, Sa - ra - spon - da, Ret - set - set!

Ah - do - ray - oh!   Ah - do - ray - boom - day - oh!

Ah - do - ray - boom - day, Ret - set - set!   Ah - say - pa - say - oh!

● Find *do'* in this song.

My Hat *(Mein Hut)*

German Folk Song

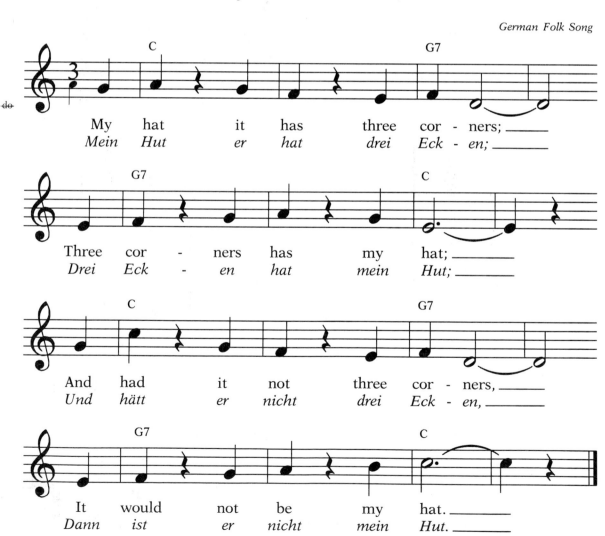

My	hat	it	has	three	cor -	ners; _____
Mein	*Hut*	*er*	*hat*	*drei*	*Eck -*	*en;* _____

Three	cor -	ners	has	my	hat; _____	
Drei	*Eck -*	*en*	*hat*	*mein*	*Hut;* _____	

And	had	it	not	three	cor -	ners, _____
Und	*hätt*	*er*	*nicht*	*drei*	*Eck -*	*en,* _____

It	would	not	be	my	hat. _____	
Dann	*ist*	*er*	*nicht*	*mein*	*Hut.* _____	

My

hat

three

corners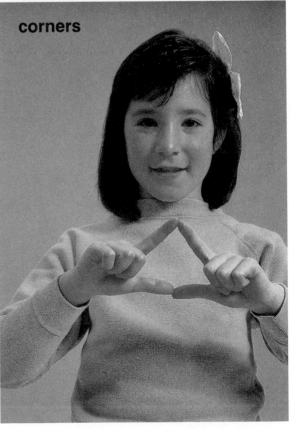

99

PLAYING THE RECORDER

- Hold your recorder in the position shown in this picture. The left hand goes on the top, the right hand on the bottom.
- Press your fingers and thumb over the holes as shown. The holes should make a light mark on your fingertips.
- Cover the tip of the mouthpiece with your lips.
- Blow gently into the recorder.

● Use your fingers to play **B A G** on the recorder.

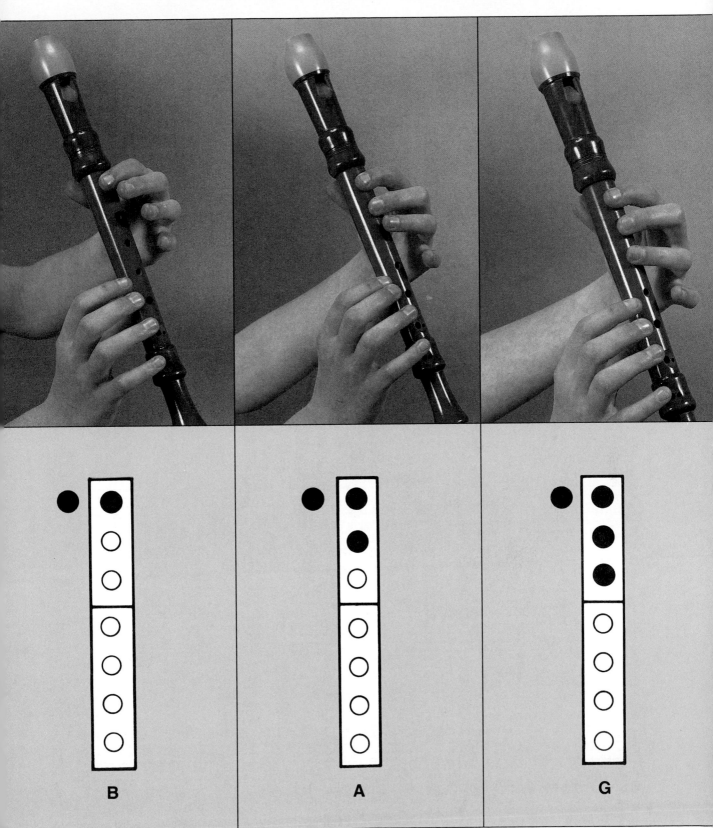

B   A   G

A BALLAD ABOUT A FOX

A **ballad** is a song that tells a story.

● As you listen to "The Fox," think about the story.

The Fox

American Folk Song

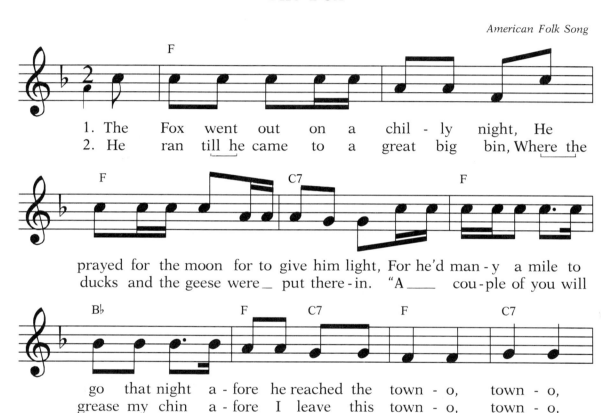

1. The Fox went out on a chil-ly night, He
2. He ran till he came to a great big bin, Where the

prayed for the moon for to give him light, For he'd man-y a mile to
ducks and the geese were _ put there-in. "A ___ cou-ple of you will

go that night a-fore he reached the town-o, town-o,
grease my chin a-fore I leave this town-o, town-o,

town-o, he'd man-y a mile to go that night A-
town-o, A cou-ple of you will grease my chin A-

fore he reached the town-o. _____
fore I leave this town-o." _____

3. He grabbed the gray goose by the neck;
   Threw a duck across his back.
   He didn't mind their quack, quack, quack
   And their legs all dangling down-o.
   Down-o, down-o.
   He didn't mind their quack, quack, quack
   And their legs all dangling down-o.

4. Then old Mother Flipper-Flopper jumped out of bed.
   Out of the window she cocked her head,
   Crying, "John, John! The gray goose is gone
   And the fox is on the town-o!
   Town-o, town-o!"
   Crying, "John, John! The gray goose is gone
   And the fox is on the town-o!

5. Then John he went to the top of the hill;
   Blew his horn both loud and shrill;
   The fox he said, "I'd better flee with my kill
   Or they'll soon be on my trail-o!
   Trail-o, trail-o!"
   The fox he said, "I'd better flee with my kill
   Or they'll soon be on my trail-o!"

6. He ran till he came to his cozy den,
   There were the little ones, eight, nine, ten.
   They said, "Daddy, better go back again
   'Cause it must be a mighty fine town-o!
   Town-o, town-o!"
   They said, "Daddy, better go back again
   'Cause it must be a mighty fine town-o!"

7. Then the fox and his wife without any strife,
   Cut up the goose with a fork and knife;
   They never had such a supper in their life
   And the little ones chewed on the bones-o.
   Bones-o, bones-o.
   They never had such a supper in their life
   And the little ones chewed on the bones-o.

INTRODUCING LOW *la*

Won't You Let the Birdie Out?

Written and adapted
by Bessie Jones

Group 1 / G
Is this door locked? _ (No, child, no.) Is this door locked? _

(No, child, no.) Won't you let the bird-ie out? (No, child, no.) Won't you

let your bird-ie out? _ (No, child, no.) I'll give you a piece of sweet bread.

(No, child, no.) I'll give you a piece of bis-cuit. (No, child, no.)

You can also write low *la* like this: *la*, or this: 6,.

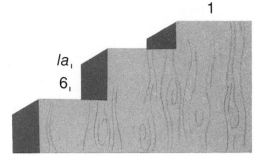

- Sing down from *do* to find *la*,.

- Sing *do*   *do*.
      la,

- Play the *do*   *do* tune on the bells.
      la,

Which words in "Won't You Let the Birdie Out?" match this tune?

Spirituals are songs that have a religious or spiritual meaning. The oldest spirituals were not written down but passed on from singer to singer. Spirituals were first sung by Africans brought to America as slaves. Spirituals can be slow or fast. Often there is hand clapping with the music. Spirituals can be sung by a soloist or a soloist and chorus.

"Train Is A-Coming" is sung by a soloist and group.

This type of song is called **call and response.**

● Listen to "Train Is A-Coming." Then make up some of your own verses.

Train Is A-Coming

African American Spiritual

● Raise your hand when you hear *la,* *do.*

6, 1

INTRODUCING LOW *so*

- Listen to this song about Martin Luther King, Jr.
- Find the lowest pitch in this song as you sing the echo parts. This pitch is called low *so* (*so,* or 5,).

Sing About Martin

*Words and music by
"Miss Jackie" Weisman*

Sing a-bout Mar - tin (sing a-bout Mar - tin) Sing a-bout

car - ing (sing a-bout car - ing) Sing a-bout peace (sing a-bout

peace) All a-round the world (all a-round the world) Sing a-bout

Mar - tin (sing a-bout Mar - tin) Sing a-bout lov - ing (sing a-bout

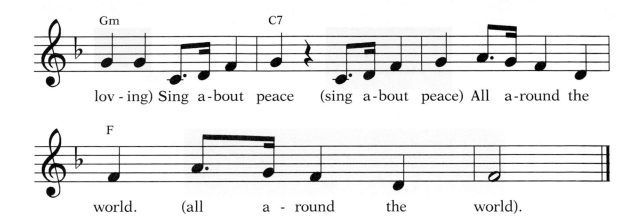

lov - ing) Sing a-bout peace (sing a-bout peace) All a-round the

world. (all a - round the world).

In "Sonata for Violin and Piano" one instrument
copies or echoes the other. This is called **imitation.**

● Listen to "Sonata for Violin and Piano." Which
instrument plays first? Which is the echo?

 "Sonata for Violin and Piano," Fourth Movement, by
César Franck

Instrument 1

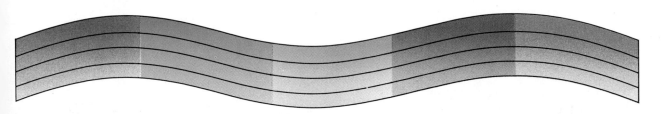

Instrument 2

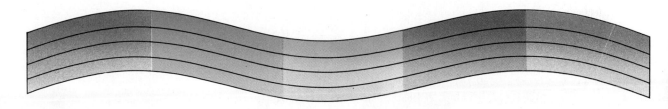

● Play a singing game with this song.

Turn the Glasses Over

American Singing Game

Verse

do

F   C7   F   C7

I've been to Haar - lem, I've been to Do - ver,

F

I've trav - eled this wide world all o - ver,

F   C7

O - ver, o - ver, three times o - ver,

F   C7   F

Drink what you have to drink and turn the glass - es o - ver.

Refrain

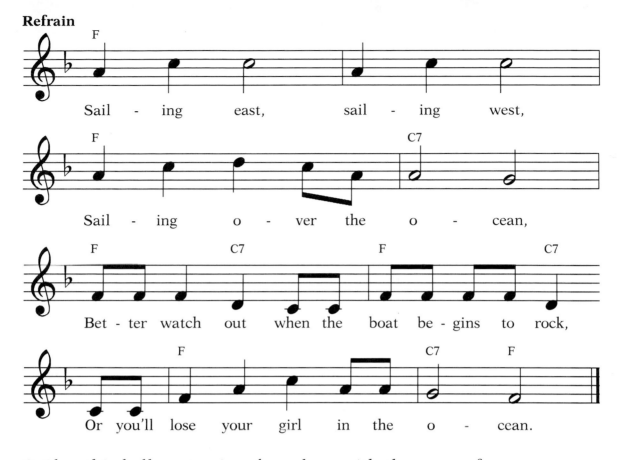

Sail - ing east, sail - ing west,

Sail - ing o - ver the o - cean,

Bet - ter watch out when the boat be - gins to rock,

Or you'll lose your girl in the o - cean.

● Play this bell part using *do* and *so,* with the verse of "Turn the Glasses Over."

Which measure is different from the others?

PLAYING G A B ON THE RECORDER

- Use your left hand to cover the holes. Support the recorder with your right hand.

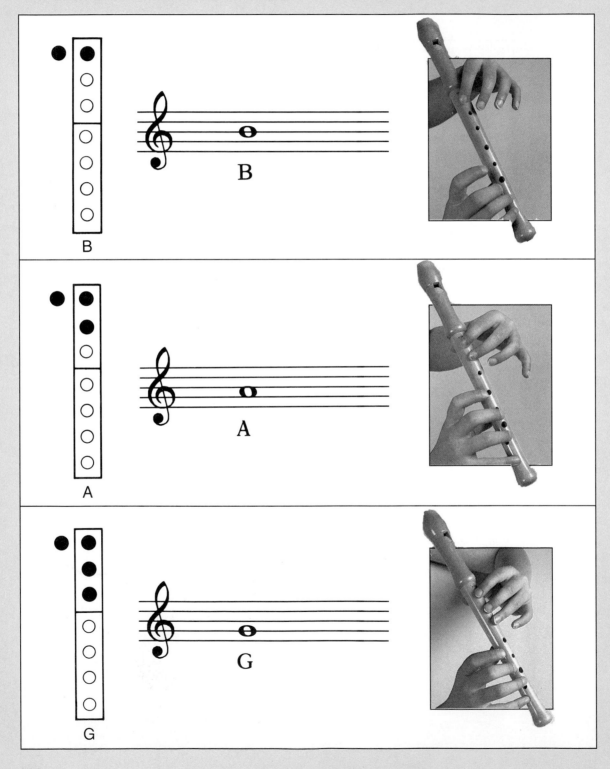

B

A

G

● Sing and play this song.

Hot Cross Buns

Traditional

Hot cross buns, hot cross buns, one-a-pen-ny, two-a-pen-ny, hot cross buns.

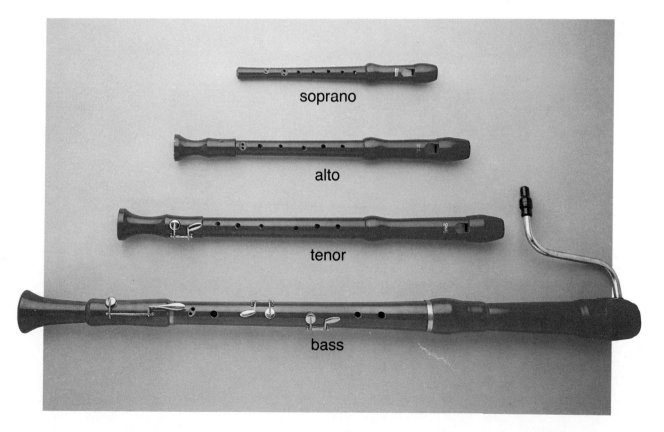

soprano

alto

tenor

bass

This picture shows different sizes of recorders. Recorders can be made of wood or plastic.

113

FAST AND SLOW

● Listen to the poem. Decide which train picture
matches the tempo for each verse.

Trains at Night

I like the whistle of trains at night,
The fast trains thundering by so proud!
They rush and rumble across the world.
They ring wild bells and they toot so loud!

But I love better the slower trains.
They take their time through the world instead,
And whistle softly and stop to tuck
Each sleepy blinking town in bed!

—*Frances M. Frost*

Train du soir/Trains du soir, Paul Delvaux, MUSÉES ROYAUX DES BEAUX-ARTS DE BELGIQUE, Brussels

Objects that are near are shown larger than objects
that are farther away in this painting.
Notice how the lines draw together to show distance.

114

The Train

Words and music by Fran Addicott

Hear that train go click - e - ty clack

Toot - in' its whis - tle and blow - in' its stack.

Hear that train go click - e - ty clack

Go - ing some - where, ain't com - in' ___ back.

- Listen for the changes in the tempo. Rub your hands or play an instrument on the beat. Get faster or slower as the tempo changes.

 "Hungarian Dance No. 5," by Johannes Brahms

VIOLIN TONE COLOR

The violin is usually played by drawing the bow across the strings. This is called **arco.** When this is done smoothly, the violin makes a lovely singing sound.

arco

Sometimes the violin is played by plucking the strings with a finger. This is called **pizzicato.**

pizzicato

● Listen as Corey Cerovsek plays both arco and pizzicato in these two pieces.

 "Banjo and the Fiddle," by William Kroll
"Scherzo Tarantella," by Henryk Wieniawski

Corey Cerovsek, a talented young violinist, entered Indiana University School of Music at the age of 12. He has played with symphony orchestras in the United States, Canada, and Australia. He also likes mathematics. Corey says, "My goal is to become a world famous soloist."

The Green Violinist was painted by Marc Chagall. Its setting is a Russian village. As a child Chagall lived in a Russian village. Is this a realistic picture? What do you see that is unexpected? Have you ever drawn a fantasy picture?

SETS OF TWO OR THREE

- Point to an engine for each beat as you sing or listen to "The Train."

Are the beats grouped in sets of two or three?

- Point to a hat for each beat as you sing or listen to "My Hat."

Are the beats grouped in sets of two or three?

What groups do you see in these pictures?

The Three Musicians, Pablo Picasso, THE MUSEUM OF MODERN ART, NY

Carnival is a time to celebrate. In Venice, Italy, people dress in fancy costumes and wear masks. They go out into the square to dance and show off their costumes.

● Listen to "Variations on 'Carnival of Venice.'"

 "Variations on 'Carnival of Venice,'" by Niccolo Paganini (päg-ə-nē′ nē)

What familiar song did you hear in this music?

TRAVELING WITH MUSIC

● Review these songs by making up a story about traveling.

● Sing the songs as part of the story.

"Turn the Glasses Over"   **"Train Is A-Coming"**

"Sarasponda"   **"Welcome, Friends"**

"My Hat"   **"Sing About Martin"**

"Won't You Let the Birdie Out?"   **"All Who Born in January"**

● Point to and name orchestral stringed instruments when you hear them.

● Play and sing these pitch patterns. Then name the songs that include them.

a.
C	D	F	A	A
so,	la,	do	mi	mi
5,	6,	1	3	3

b.
F	F	F	D	C
do	do	do	la,	so,
1	1	1	6,	5,

c.
C	C'	A	G
do	do'	la	so
1	8	6	5

JUST CHECKING

See how much you remember.

1. Point to the word below which means plucked.

   a. arco   b. pizzicato

2. Point to the staff that shows *do la,* or 1 6,.

   a.    b.

3. Name the instruments pictured here.

4. Point to the staff that shows *do do'* or 1 8.

   a.    b.

5. Point to the staff that shows *do so,* or 1 5,.

   a.    b.

UNIT 6

DIFFERENT PEOPLE MAKE DIFFERENT MUSIC

MUSIC OF AFRICAN AMERICANS

A spiritual is a kind of religious song created by African Americans in the United States. The words of these songs often tell about the hope for freedom. They also can refer to events in the Bible. Where do you think the chariot will take them?

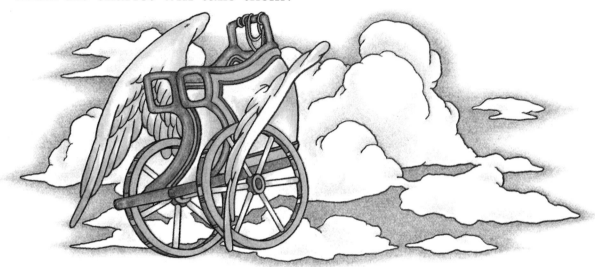

Good News

African American Spiritual

Good news! (clap clap) Char-i-ot's com-in', Good

news! (clap clap) Char-i-ot's com-in', Good news! (clap clap)

Char-i-ot's com-in' and I don't want it to leave me be-hind.

Games and dances invented by African Americans are often shared when children gather together to play. A well known composer, R. Nathaniel Dett, used the rhythms of an African American folk dance he had learned as a child in "Juba" (Dance).

R. Nathaniel Dett helped many people to find out about the music of African Americans. He directed choirs who sang spirituals for audiences in the United States and Europe.

● Tap the beat as you listen to "Juba" (Dance). Use more fingers when it is louder and fewer fingers when it is softer.

 "Juba" (Dance) from *In the Bottoms,* by R. Nathaniel Dett

● Look for loud ***f*** and soft ***p*** signs in this music from "Juba."

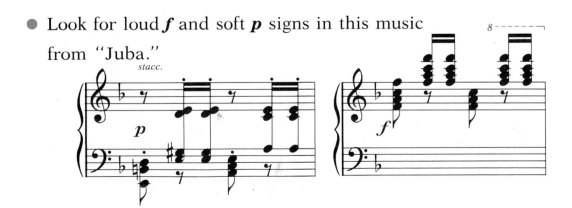

This is a singing game that children play.

Circle 'Round the Zero

*Traditional American
Playground Game*

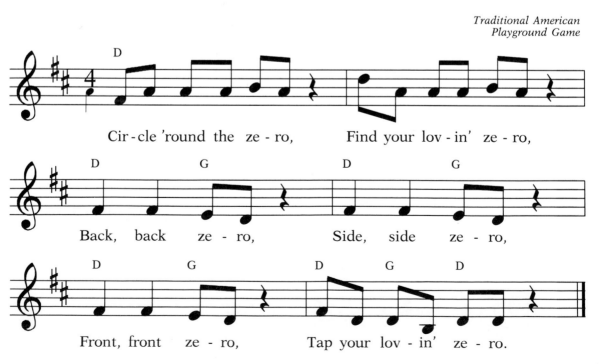

Cir-cle 'round the ze-ro,   Find your lov-in' ze-ro,

Back, back ze-ro,   Side, side ze-ro,

Front, front ze-ro,   Tap your lov-in' ze-ro.

DYNAMICS IN ART AND MUSIC

What different things are people doing in this painting?
What sounds might you hear if you were standing on
this street?

Parade on Hammond St., Allan Crite.
PHILLIPS COLLECTION, Washington, D.C.

What would make the loudest sound in this painting?
What would make the softest sound in the painting?
The louds and softs in music are called **dynamics.**

● Listen for different dynamics in "Street Song." Move
your hands apart when the music becomes louder and
closer when the music is softer.

 "Street Song," by Carl Orff

Two new dynamic levels are **very soft** and **very loud.**
Both of the pictures below show loud sounds. Which one
shows the louder sound? How do you know?

The musical term for loud is *forte*. The musical term
for very loud is **fortissimo.** The symbol for fortissimo is **ff**.

● Point to the picture above that shows
fortissimo.

The musical term for soft is *piano*. What word do you
think means very soft?

What would be the symbol for **pianissimo?**

● Point to the picture below that shows the softer sound.

Snow

A snow can come as quietly
as cats can walk across a floor.
It hangs its curtains in the air
and piles its weight against the door.
It fills old nests with whiter down
than any swan has ever known,
and then as silent as it came,
you find the pale snow bird has flown.

But snow can come quite otherwise,
with windy uproar and commotion,
with shaken trees and banging blinds,
still salty from a touch of ocean.
Such storms will wrestle with strong boys
and set the girls' skirts wildly blowing
until it throws its cap in air and shouts,
"Well, good-bye now! I'm going!"

—*Elizabeth Coatsworth*

OLD AND NEW PITCHES

What song can you name that uses just these three
pitches?

B   A   G

● Find this pattern in the song.

Chatter with the Angels

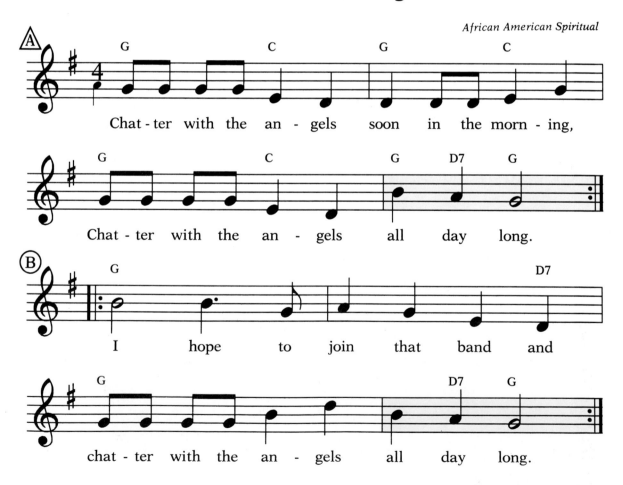

African American Spiritual

Ⓐ Chat - ter with the an - gels soon in the morn - ing,

Chat - ter with the an - gels all day long.

Ⓑ I hope to join that band and

chat - ter with the an - gels all day long.

● Play the **B A G** pattern on bells or recorder every time
it appears in the song.

Tongue-Twister Canon

Traditional Round
Words adapted

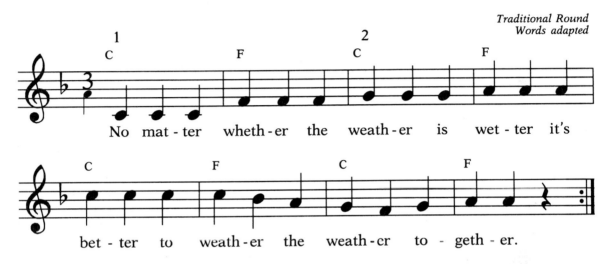

No mat - ter wheth - er the weath - er is wet - ter it's

bet - ter to weath - er the weath - er to - geth - er.

A **descant** is a melody that sounds at the same time as the main melody of a song. Below is a descant for "Tongue-Twister Canon."

Is the last note in the first line higher or lower than G? Use your answer to figure out the name of this new pitch.

PITCHES YOU KNOW

The Chinese New Year celebration lasts five days. It begins
with a quiet time shared with family and friends.
Later there is a noisy parade. It is led by a dragon
figure that can be carried by as many as 100 people.

What is unusual about the line that uses instruments only?

Song of the Dragon

Traditional Chinese
Folk Song

See the drag-on come on a hun-dred legs!

He brings us all good cheer; him we do not fear!

Long life and peace and joy in the bright New Year!

(Instruments only)

New Year, New Year, New Year is here! _____

TONE COLOR

This song is about colonial times in America.

Can you find the fermata in the song?

What instrument do you hear in "In Good Old Colony
Times"?

In Good Old Colony Times

American folk song
Words adapted by P. R. K.

1. In good old col-on-y times when we lived un-der the king,
2. O the first he was _ a mil-ler and the sec-ond he was _ a wea-ver,

Three _ rogu-ish chaps fell in-to mis-haps, be - cause they could not sing,
And the third he was a tail - or man, Three rogu - ish chaps to-ge-ther.

Refrain

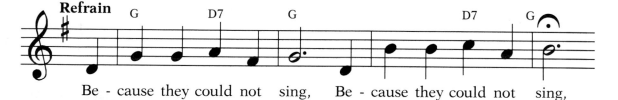

Be - cause they could not sing, Be - cause they could not sing,

Three _ rogu-ish chaps fell in-to mis-haps, be-cause they could not sing.

3. O the miller, he stole corn;
   and the weaver, he stole yarn,
   And the tailor man ran right away
   with the broadcloth under his arm.
   Refrain

4. The miller was drowned in the dam,
   and the weaver got hung in his yarn,
   And the tailor tripped as he ran away
   with the broadcloth under his arm.
   Refrain

The **harpsichord** was a popular instrument in colonial times. When a key is pressed down, a quill or small piece of leather plucks a string. The harpsichord can play only limited dynamics.

The piano was invented in 1709. It was called the **pianoforte** because it could play very soft and very loud. When a key is pressed down, strings are hit by a small hammer.

harpsichord

piano

Do you hear the piano or the harpsichord in this piece?

 "English Country Dance"

Settlers were fearful of poisonous snakes and called them "sarpents."

How can you use dynamics to tell the story of this ballad?

Springfield Mountain

American Ballad

Verse

1. On Spring-field Moun - tain there did dwell
2. One Mon - day morn - ing he did go

a hand-some youth; I knew him well. _____
down in the mea - dow for to mow. _____

Refrain

Too loo - re - ay, too loo - re - oo,

Too loo - re - ay, too loo - re - oo.

3. When he had mowed but half the field,
   a pesky sarpent bit his heel.

4. He took his scythe and with a blow,
   he laid the pesky sarpent low.

5. He took the sarpent in his hand
   and straightway went to Molly Bland.

6. "Oh, Molly, Molly, here you see
   the pesky sarpent what bit me."

7. Now, Molly had a ruby lip
   with which the pizen she did sip.

8. But Molly had a rotten tooth
   and so the pizen kill'd them both.

FINDING METER

- Clap the strong beats and touch your fingertips together on the weak beats of "English Country Dance."

What is the meter?

- Do the dance.

- Follow the meter maze. Remember that in $\frac{3}{4}$, ♩ = one beat, ♪ = two beats, ♩. = three beats, ♫ = one beat, 𝄽 = one beat of silence.

- Reach the end of the maze by following the line which connects all the patterns of three beats.

- Make a list of the letters below the patterns you choose. If your answers are correct, you will spell a word.

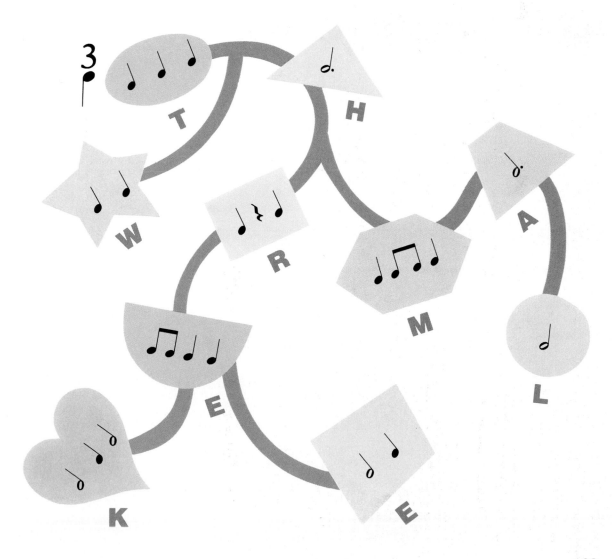

DYNAMIC DIFFERENCES

Which instrument can play both fortissimo and pianissimo?

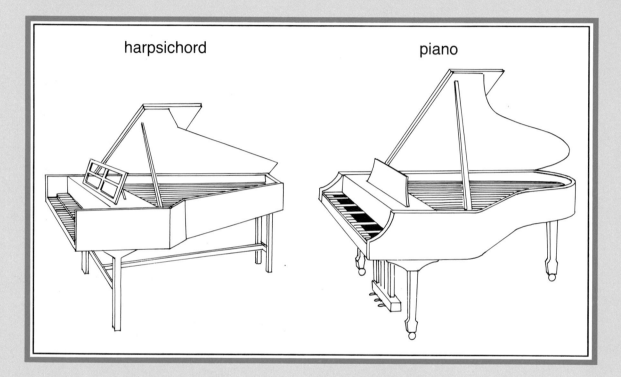

harpsichord   piano

- Sing one of these songs using your own plan for getting louder or softer.

"In Good Old Colony Times"

"Springfield Mountain"

- Sing one of these songs adding or subtracting voices to make the sound loud or soft.

"Good News"

"Circle 'Round the Zero"

JUST CHECKING

See how much you remember.

1. Match the name of the instrument with the kind of action that produces its sound.

   piano   harpsichord

   a. quill plucking string

   b. hammer striking string

2. How does each action affect the sound?

3. Point to the word that means very loud.

   a. forte   b. piano

   c. pianissimo   d. fortissimo

4. Which line shows the dynamic symbols in order from very soft to very loud?

   a. *pp p ff f*

   b. *pp p f ff*

   c. *p pp f ff*

   d. *p pp ff f*

UNIT 7 STRINGS IN SPRING

PHRASES IN MUSIC

A **phrase** is a musical thought.

- Find the long and short phrases in this song.
  The phrase marks will help you.
- Pretend to pet a large animal as you sing "Animal
  Fair." Pet the animal's head during the short phrases.
  Pet the animal's whole body on the long phrases.

Animal Fair

Traditional American Folk Song

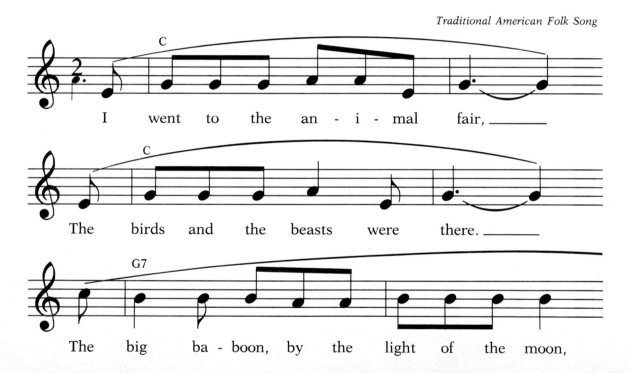

I went to the an - i - mal fair, _____

The birds and the beasts were there. _____

The big ba - boon, by the light of the moon,

was comb-ing his au-burn hair. _____

You ought to have seen the monk; _____

He climbed up the el-e-phant's trunk. _____

The el-e-phant sneezcd and fell on her knees,

and what be-came of the monk?

The **string bass** is the largest stringed instrument that is played with a bow. The player sits on a tall stool or stands. Sometimes the string bass is called the double bass or bass viol. It makes very low sounds. Camille Saint-Säens (saN-säN′) wrote *Carnival of the Animals* to describe different animals in sound.

string bass

● Listen for the string bass and the long and short phrases.

 "The Elephant" from *Carnival of the Animals,* by Camille Saint-Saëns

What instrument is playing the part of the elephant?

A **cello** is a stringed instrument smaller than the
string bass. It makes low sounds but not as low as the
string bass. The cello rests on a long end pin.
A person plays the cello sitting down.

● Identify the instrument playing the melody of "The
Swan."

 "The Swan" from *Carnival of the Animals,*
by Camille Saint-Saëns

Were the phrases in the music long or short?

cello

● Say the French names for the parts of the bird shown here.

le bec (the beak)

le nez (the nose)

la tête (the head)

le dos (the back)

le cou (the neck)

les pattes (the claws)

- Find the two phrases in the refrain.
- Sing "Alouette." Point to the parts of your body as you sing.

Alouette

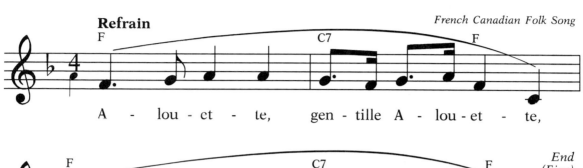

Refrain   *French Canadian Folk Song*

A - lou - et - te,   gen - tille A - lou - et - te,

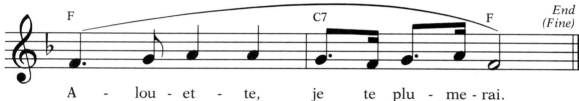

End (Fine)

A - lou - et - te,   je   te   plu - me - rai.

Verse

Leader   Group

1. Je   te plu - me - rai   la tête,   Je   te plu - me - rai   la tête,
2. Je   te plu - me - rai   le bec,   Je   te plu - me - rai   le bec.

Leader   Group   *(No repeat first time)*   Go back to the beginning and sing to the End. *(Da Capo al Fine)*

1. Et   la tête, et   la tête.
2. { Et   le bec, et   le bec.   A - lou - ette, A - lou - ette.   Oh!
   { Et   la tête, et   la tête.

3. Le nez   4. Le dos   5. Les pattes   6. Le cou

"Alouette, Gentille Alouette" performed by Saint-Laurent Children's Choir

THE WHOLE NOTE AND WHOLE REST

The **whole note** (o) sounds for four beats. The **whole rest** (▬) stands for four beats of silence.

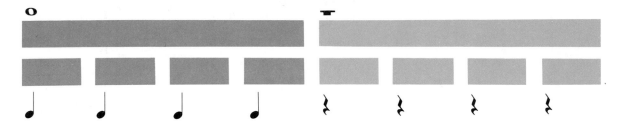

● Find the whole notes (o) in the song.

If All Men Would Live as Brothers

Words and music by Michael Lane

If all men would live as broth-ers, what a good world this would be.

Live   as   broth   -   ers,   what a hap - py   world!

Live   as   broth   -   ers,   what a hap - py   world!

● Play these patterns with "If All Men Would Live as Brothers." Use the Gm button on the Autoharp or play the note G on the piano or resonator bells.

150

- Listen to this poem. It is read without a steady beat.
- Now say the poem with a steady beat. How many beats are in each line of the poem?
- Play whole notes on a ringing instrument as you read this poem.

I Am a Leprechaun

I am a leprechaun.
Catch me if you can!
Now you see me, now you don't,
Catch me where I am.

In and out, up and down,
Chase me through the streets of town.
Chase me fast, chase me slow,
Chase me middle, high, and low.
Chase me over, under, round,
Chase me soft without a sound.
Chase me loud like thunder's din,
Chase me, chase me, you won't win!

I am a leprechaun.
Catch me if you can!
Now you see me, now you don't,
Catch me where I am!

—*John Horman*

USING B A G

● Find the pitch pattern **B B A A G** in this song.

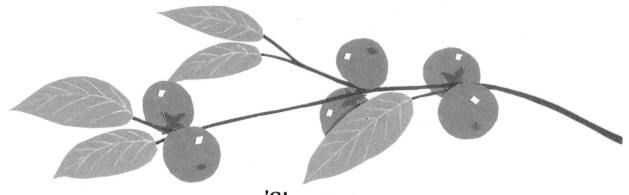

'Simmons

Alabama Singing Game

1. Cir-cle left, do oh, do oh, cir-cle left, do oh, do oh,
2. Cir-cle right, do oh, do oh, cir-cle right, do oh, do oh,

Cir-cle left, do oh, do oh, Shake them 'sim-mons down!
Cir-cle right, do oh, do oh, Shake them 'sim-mons down!

3. Balance all, do oh, do oh, . . .

4. 'Round your partners, do oh, do oh, . . .

5. 'Round your corners, do oh, do oh, . . .

6. Prom'nade all, do oh, do oh, . . .

● Make up patterns using B A G to play on recorders or bells.

● Play these patterns between the verses of this song.

152

● Learn the dance for "'Simmons."

RHYTHM AND METER

● Find the whole notes in this song.

Kayak Song

Traditional Inuit Song
Translated by Emily I. Brown
Transcribed and arranged by Roxie K. Bergh

Roll-ing, roll-ing, Roll-ing, roll-ing, Roll-ing o'er the waves.

Roll-ing, roll-ing, Roll-ing, roll-ing, Roll-ing o'er the waves.

Pad-dling as I go, turn-ing to the shore,

It is fun to learn and see the wa-ter churn.

● Feel the strong beat as you paddle to the pictures below.

Which picture below shows the meter of "Kayak Song"?

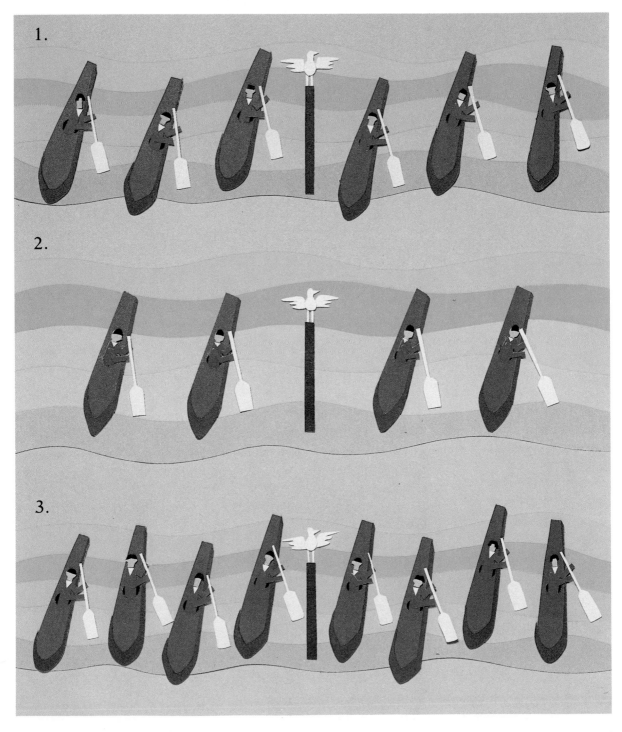

KEYBOARD ORDER

When all the resonator bells are in their case, they look like a piano keyboard.

The resonator bells have groups of two and three black bells.

- Point to a group of two black bells.
- Point to the group of three black bells.

Are G A and B closer to a group of two or a group of three black bells?

Here are G A B on the staff.

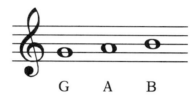

G   A   B

The piano keyboard also has groups of two and three black keys.

● Point to all of the G A and B keys.

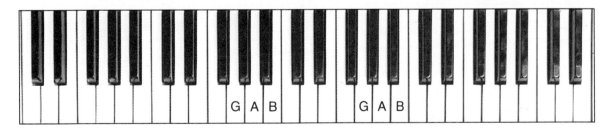

● Listen to the sound of the piano.

"Polonaise in A major," Op. 40, No. 1 (opening section), by Frederic Chopin (shō´paN)

- Find the pattern of B B A A G in this song. Sometimes this pattern is made longer by repeating some of the pitches.
- Find the B B A A G patterns which have repeated notes.
- Play these pitches on the B A G bells or the piano.

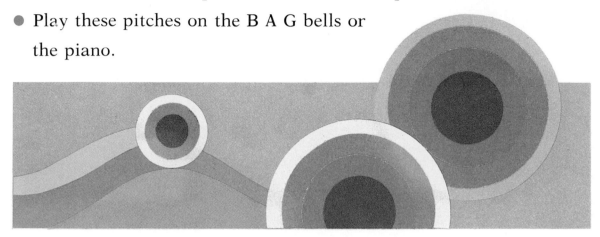

Ezekiel Saw the Wheel

Spiritual

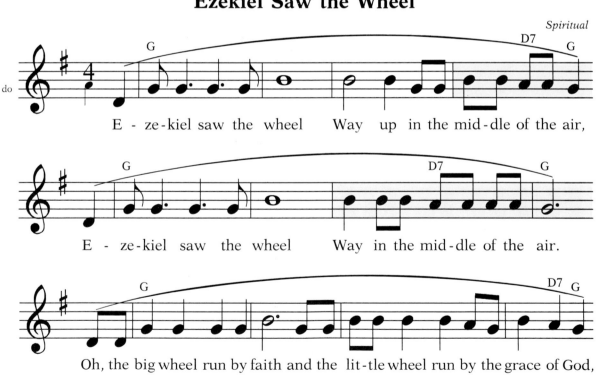

E - ze-kiel saw the wheel Way up in the mid-dle of the air,

E - ze-kiel saw the wheel Way in the mid-dle of the air.

Oh, the big wheel run by faith and the lit-tle wheel run by the grace of God,

A wheel in a wheel Way in the mid-dle of the air.

MORE STRINGS

The **viola** is a stringed instrument that is a little larger than the violin. It has a lower sound than the violin. It is held under the chin.

viola

● Listen to the sound of the viola.

 "Presto" (fourth movement) from *Concerto in G Major,* by Georg Philipp Telemann

● Find the whole notes (o) and whole rests (⬮) in this song.

Nature's Sweet Endless Song

Words and music by Hap Palmer

1. Waves are roll-ing, _ slow-ly mov-ing in and mov-ing out. _
2. Wa - ter ris - ing, _ ris - ing up to form the clouds so high. _

Waves are roll-ing, _ slow - ly mov-ing in and mov-ing out. _
Then it's fall-ing, _ rain-drops fall - ing down to give us life. _

In and out, __ shift-ing sands, _ ev-er on and on,
Rise and fall, __ up and down, _ ev-er on and on,

just sing - ing na-ture's sweet end-less __ song. ____
just sing - ing na-ture's sweet end-less __ song. ____

Earth is turn-ing _ through the seas-ons, turn-ing 'round and 'round.
Flow-ers o - pen, _ Show their col - or to the morn-ing sun. __

Earth is turn-ing __ through the seas-ons, turn-ing 'round and 'round. __
Give their pol - len, __ then they close up when their work is done. __

Day and night, __ dark and light, __ ev-er on and on,
O - pen, close, __ live and die, __ ev-er on and on,

End
(Fine)

just sing - ing na-ture's sweet end - less __ song. __
just sing - ing na-ture's sweet end - less __ song. __

The riv - er flows, it curves and turns;

Go to the beginning and sing to the End.
(Da Capo al Fine)

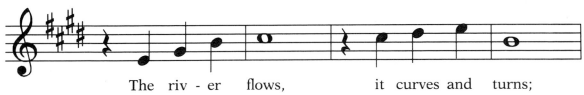

then it straight-ens and bends a-gain, __ wind-ing on __ to the sea. __

MOVING IN PHRASES

- Follow the phrase marks as you sing the song.

- Draw an arc in the air on each phrase.

April Fool's Day

Words and music by Wayne Chadwick

1. If you ev - er have a day when your friends all say your shoe-lace is un-tied,

And a big green bug with thir-teen legs is crawl-ing up your side,

Don't let it both - er you or fill you with dis - may!

If you ev - er have a cra-zy kind of day like that, it's A-pril Fool's Day!

2. If the present that your best friend
offers you turns out to be a fake,
And when you open up the box
out jumps a springy snake,
Don't let it frighten you
and turn your hair to gray,
If you ever get a silly kind of gift
like that, it's April Fool's Day!

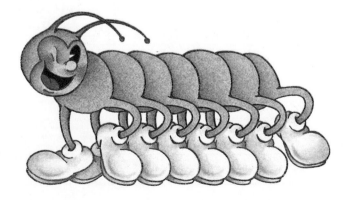

SAME AND DIFFERENT PHRASES

● Look at the music to find which phrase is different
from the others.

Au Clair de la Lune

French Folk Song

1. Au clair de la lu - ne, Mon a - mi Pier - rot,
2. Au clair de la lu - ne, Pier - rot ré - pon - dit,

Prê - te moi ta plu - me, Pour é - crire un mot.
"Je n'ai pas de plu - me, Je suis dans mon lit.

Ma chan - delle est mor - te, Je n'ai plus de feu;
Va chez la voi - si - ne, Je crois qu'elle y est,

Ou - vre moi ta por - te, Pour l'a - mour de Dieu.
car dans sa cui - si - ne, On bat le bri - quet."

MUSIC OF HAWAII

In the 1800s, sailors from Portugal brought a small stringed instrument to the Hawaiian islands. The Hawaiians called the instrument a **ukulele.** It looks like a small guitar but it has only four strings. It is strummed like the guitar. The ukulele comes in different sizes. A small ukulele makes a higher sound than a large ukulele. The soprano ukulele plays higher sounds than the baritone.

soprano ukulele   baritone ukulele

● Listen for the sound of the ukuleles.

Kapulu Kane

Traditional Hawaiian Folk Song

Ka - pu - lu, pu - lu ka - ne, Ka - pu - lu, pu - lu ka - ne,

Ka pu - lu, Pu - lu ka - ne ku - ka - na - lu - a.

Ka pu - lu, pu - lu ka - ne, Ka - pu - lu, pu - lu ka - ne,

Ka pu - lu, Pu - lu ka - ne ku - ka - na - lu - a.

You can play this game.

These are Hawaiian rhythm instruments.

puili (split bamboo sticks) ipu (gourd drum) uli-uli (feathered gourds)

- Look for classroom instruments that are similar to these instruments.

- Shake this pattern on the uli-uli (or maracas):

- Tap this pattern on the puili (or rhythm sticks):

- Play this pattern on the ipu (or a large plastic bottle):

Play the notes with stems down with the heel of the hand.
Play the notes with the stems up with the fingertips.
Music, dance, drama, and movement were used to tell
the stories of the people of ancient Hawaii. People
remembered the past this way because the Hawaiians
did not have a written language.

166

PITCH

How many different pitches are in this song?

"Kahuli Calling" is an ancient Hawaiian hula chant. The **hula** uses hand and body movements to tell the same story as the words of the song.

Kahuli Calling

Ancient Hawaiian Chant

Ka - hu - li a - ku, Ka - hu - li mai,
Ka - hu - li call - ing, Hear us a - far,

Ka - hu - li lei u - la, lei a - ko - le - a,
A dain - ty lei made of green, love - ly fern. __

Ko - le a - ko - le - a, Ho - i - ka wai,
Of green, love - ly fern, __ Fetch us some dew,

Wai a - ko - le - a, Ko - le - a, Ko - le - a.
Dew from the fern, __ Ko - le - a, Ko - le - a.

REMEMBERING TOGETHER

● Name two songs that talk about animals.

● Sing "If All Men Would Live as Brothers." Play the patterns on the page.

● Sing "Ezekiel Saw the Wheel" and "Nature's Sweet Endless Song." Raise your hand when you hear a whole note.

● Listen again to parts of "The Elephant" and "The Swan" by Saint-Säens and "Presto" by Telemann. Look at the pictures below. Point to the instruments you hear in each song.

cello

soprano ukulele

viola

string bass

baritone ukulele

● Name the instruments you hear in the introduction to "Kapulu Kane" and then sing the song.

JUST CHECKING

1. Which note is a whole note?

   a. b. 𝅘𝅥 c. ♪ d. 𝅗𝅥

2. The whole rest is silent for how many beats in  ?

   a. one   b. four   c. eight   d. zero

3. Name the instruments in the pictures below.

   a.   b.   c.

4. Which instrument is a folk instrument used in Hawaii?

   a. viola   b. cello   c. ukulele   d. violin

5. Which comes first in this rhythm pattern?

   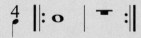

   a. whole rest   b. whole note

6. Which picture shows the correct order of the black keys on a piano?

   a.    b.

CARNIVAL OF THE ANIMALS

Camille Saint-Saëns was a French musician. He wrote music about the animals and other characters that you see below. He called it *Carnival of the Animals*.

- Listen to *Carnival of the Animals*. Match each piece of music to the correct picture and title.

 Carnival of the Animals, by Camille Saint-Saëns

● Think of how these animals move. Move to the music as the animals might move to the music from *Carnival of the Animals*. Will your movement be smooth or choppy? Fast or slow? High or low?

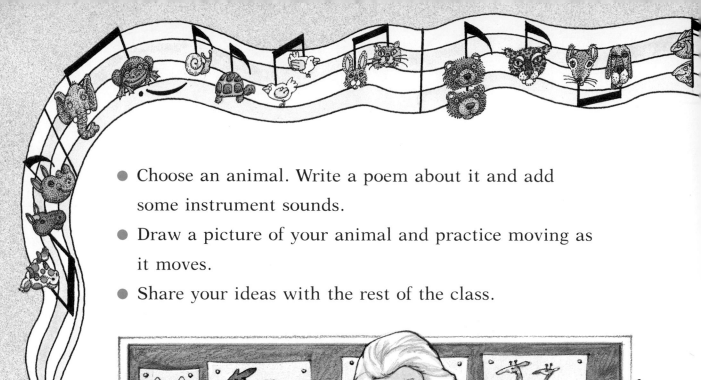

- Choose an animal. Write a poem about it and add some instrument sounds.
- Draw a picture of your animal and practice moving as it moves.
- Share your ideas with the rest of the class.

Here is a famous picture with animals.

● Find the center of interest in the picture.

In art you see the center of interest. In music you hear it. A musical center of interest is called a **climax**.

● Listen for the climax in "The Swan."

The Peaceable Kingdom, Edward Hicks, Private Collection

This painting is called *The Peaceable Kingdom.*
The artist shows many animals getting along with each other.

UNIT 8 STRINGED INSTRUMENTS FROM OTHER LANDS

MELODIC SHAPE

Shape is the outline of something.

- Trace your finger around some of the shapes on this page.

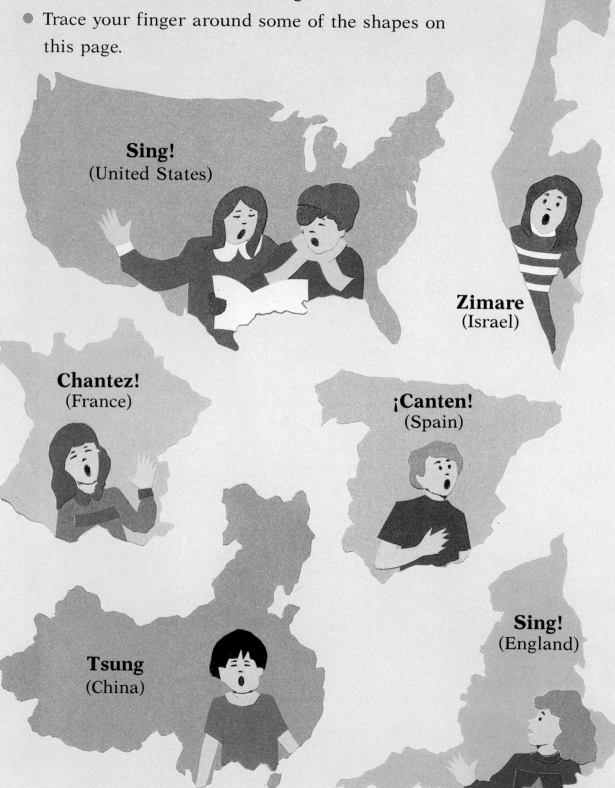

Sing!
(United States)

Zimare
(Israel)

Chantez!
(France)

¡Canten!
(Spain)

Sing!
(England)

Tsung
(China)

● Follow the notes on the blue line with
your finger as you sing the first phrase.

What other phrase has the same shape?

Sing!
(Sign language)

Sing Together

Traditional Round

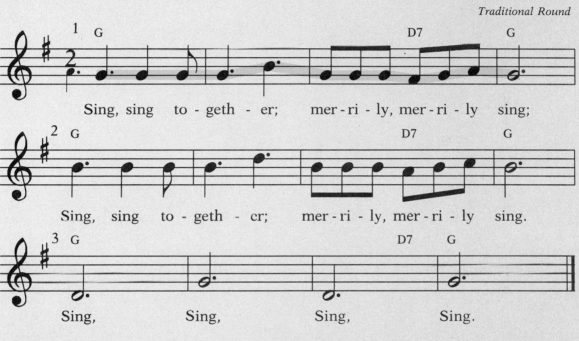

Sing, sing to - geth - er; mer - ri - ly, mer - ri - ly sing;

Sing, sing to - geth - cr; mer - ri - ly, mer - ri - ly sing.

Sing,   Sing,   Sing,   Sing.

Поёте
(Soviet Union)

Sing!
(Ghana)

● Follow the musical stairway up and down as you
listen to "Ebeneezer Sneezer."
Are all the steps the same size?

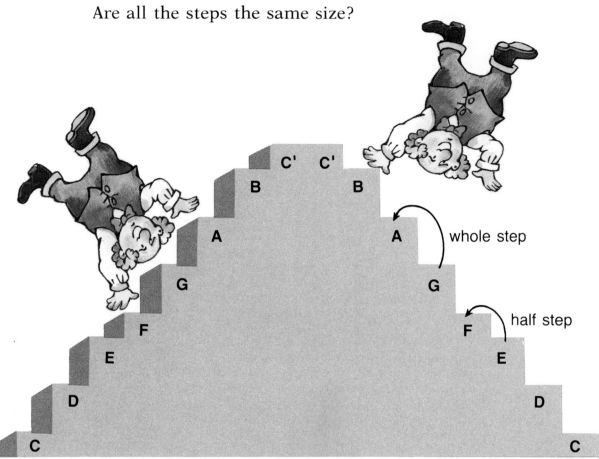

whole step

half step

- Follow the shape of the melody as you sing this song. The notes get higher with each measure and then quickly get lower at the end.

Ebeneezer Sneezer

Words and music by
Lynn Freeman Olson

E - be - nee - zer Sneez - er, ___ Top - sy - tur - vy man,

Walks up - on his el - bows ___ Ev - 'ry - time he can,

Dress - es up in pa - per ___ Ev - 'ry - time it pours,

Whis - tles "Yan - kee Doo - dle" ___ Ev - 'ry - time he snores.

Oh, E - be - nee - zer, what a man!

The **harp** is one of the oldest instruments in history. Art from the time of the Pharaohs of Egypt shows people playing the harp. Early harps look different from harps of today. Many of the earliest harps were small enough to be held on the player's lap. Today the concert harp is a large instrument with forty-seven strings and seven pedals. It is played as a solo instrument and in the orchestra.

Detail from *Female Harpist Under a Grape Arbor,* (fragment of an Egyptian leather hanging). METROPOLITAN MUSEUM OF ART, NY

harp

The harpist can pluck one string or several strings at a time. This makes it possible for the harp to play both melodies and chords.

● Listen for the sound of the harp in "Waltz of the Flowers" by Tchaikovsky. Show the melodic shape with your hand.

The harp can be played to create many different sounds. In "Chanson dans la Nuit" which means "Song in the Night" you will hear different harp sounds. The pictures below suggest the three sections of this music.

● Tell what you think the music might sound like in each part.

● Listen to hear if the music fits your words. How is the harp played to create these different sounds?

 "Chanson dans la Nuit," by Carlos Salzedo

WHOLE STEPS AND HALF STEPS

The keyboard below will help you find half steps
and whole steps.

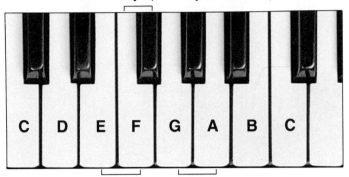

half step (no key between)

half step (no key between)   **whole step** (one key between)

- Name two pairs of white keys that are a half step
  apart.
- Find a pair of keys that are a whole step apart.

If you play two keys that are a whole step apart the
difference in sound is greater than that for two keys a
half step apart.

Which examples below show whole steps?

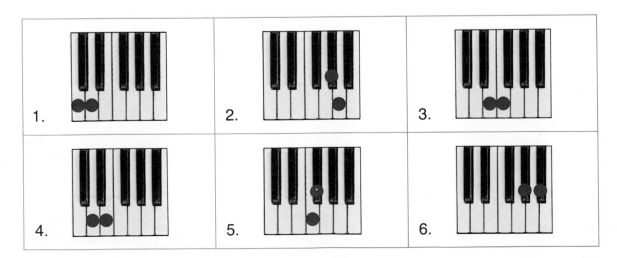

A **sharp** (♯) makes a pitch sound a half step higher.

● Find the sharp in this song.

Supercalifragilisticexpialidocious

Words by Richard M. Sherman
Music by Robert B. Sherman

1. Su-per-cal-i-frag-il-is-tic-ex-pi-al-i-do-cious!
2. Su-per-cal-i-frag-il-is-tic-ex-pi-al-i-do-cious!

E-ven though the sound of it is some-thing quite a-tro-cious,
Su-per-cal-i-frag-il-is-tic-ex-pi-al-i-do-cious!

If you say it loud e-nough, you'll al-ways sound pre-co-cious.
Su-per-cal-i-frag-il-is-tic-ex-pi-al-i-do-cious!

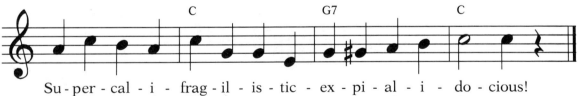

Su-per-cal-i-frag-il-is-tic-ex-pi-al-i-do-cious!
Su-per-cal-i-frag-il-is-tic-ex-pi-al-i-do-cious!

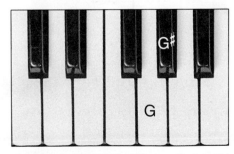

On a keyboard, a pitch is sharped by playing the very next key to the right. G♯ is a half step higher than G.

A **flat** (♭) makes a pitch sound a half step lower.

● Find the flats in the song.

Shepherd, Shepherd

African American Spiritual

1. Shep - herd, shep - herd, where'd you lose your sheep?
2. Shep - herd, shep - herd, where'd you leave your lambs?

Shep - herd, shep - herd, where'd you lose your sheep?
Shep - herd, shep - herd, where'd you leave your lambs?

Shep - herd, shep - herd, where'd you lose your sheep?
Shep - herd, shep - herd, where'd you leave your lambs?

O the sheep all gone a - stray, _____
O the sheep all gone a - stray, _____

the sheep all gone __ a - stray. _____
the sheep all gone __ a - stray. _____

On a keyboard, a pitch is flatted by playing the very next key to the left. A♭ is a half step lower than A.

184

TEXTURE TIME

Texture is the pattern of musical sound formed when different pitches are played or sung together.

● Point to the picture that shows what you hear in these songs: "Supercalifragilisticexpialidocious," "Sing Together," and "Shepherd, Shepherd."

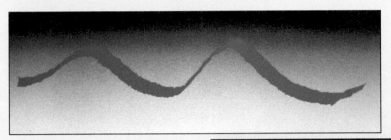

Melody alone

Melody with chord accompaniment

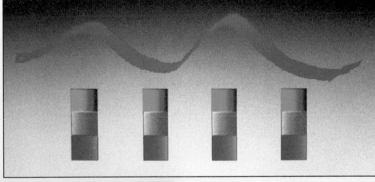

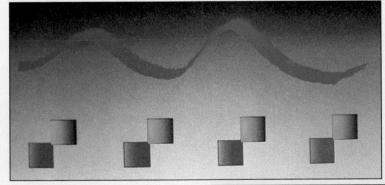

Melody with ostinato accompaniment

Melody in canon

WATCH YOUR STEP— AND HALF STEPS TOO

- Play "Ebeneezer Sneezer" starting on different pitches.

- Start on G. Play the letters above the keyboard. The half steps are between B and C, and F♯ and G.
- Start on F. Play the letters below the keyboard. The half steps are between A and B♭, and E and F.

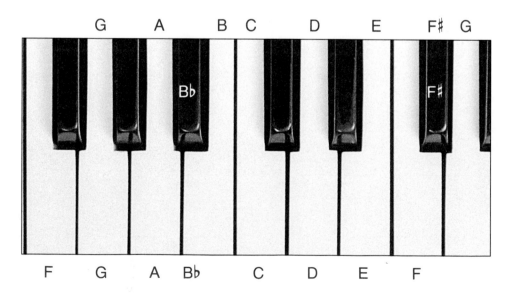

You can play part of "Shepherd, Shepherd" on the bells.

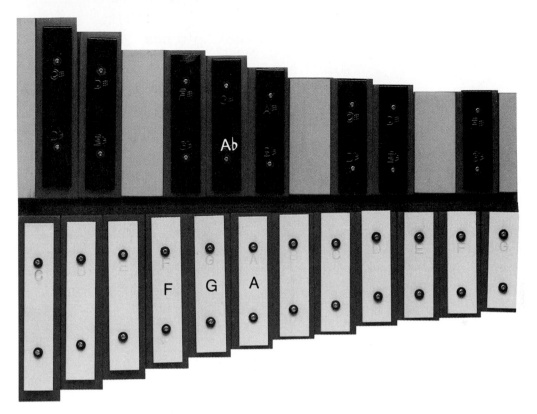

● Point to the bells you need to play each of these
patterns.

1.

Ab G   F
lose your sheep

2.

A   G   F
O   the sheep

PITCHES ON A HAND STAFF

You can use your hand to show pitches.

Your fingers are the lines.

so(5) C

mi(3) A

do(1) F

● Use the hand staff to practice
naming pitches you have learned.

● Find the notes that look like this:

You speak the words for these notes instead of singing them.

Tue, Tue

Folk Song from Ghana

On what three pitches are the words *Tue, Tue* sung?

● Point to those pitches on your hand staff.

Detail from: *Streams and Hills under Fresh Snow,* Anonymous Chinese handscroll.
THE METROPOLITAN MUSEUM OF ART, NY

Spring in China

Chinese Folk Song

Spring brings the sun - shine to melt win - ter's snow.

Spring brings the warm __ rains to help flow - ers grow.

Spring brings song - birds from far a __ way;

Joy - ful mu - sic is heard all __ day,

Min - gling with laugh - ter as chil - dren __ play.

Detail from *Finches and Bamboo*, Hui-tsung, Chinese handscroll, THE METROPOLITAN MUSEUM OF ART, NY

Detail from *Wang Hsi-chih Watching Geese*, Ch'ien Hsüan, Chinese handscroll, THE METROPOLITAN MUSEUM OF ART, NY

Do (1) can be on any line or space of the staff.

If *do* is on a line, *mi* is on the line above, and *so* is on the line above that.

If *do* is in a space, *mi* is in the space above and *so* is in the space above that. In this song *do* (1) is on the first line.

● Tell where *mi* (3) and *so* (5) are.

● Point to the pitches of "Spring in China" on your hand staff as you sing the song.

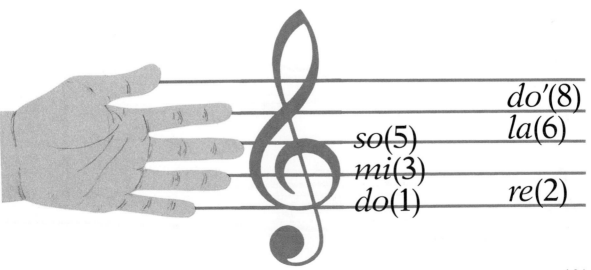

191

2. METER

Use these words from "Sing Together" to help you read the rhythm of the A section in this song:

For every ♩. say *sing*.

For every ♩♪♪ say *merrily*.

Oh, Dear, What Can the Matter Be?

English Folk Song

Oh, dear, what can the mat - ter be?

Dear, dear, what can the mat - ter be?

Oh, dear, what can the mat - ter be?

John - ny's so long at the Fair.

He prom-ised to bring me a bas-ket of po-sies,

A wreath of white lil-ies, a wreath of red ros-es,

A lit-tle straw hat to set off the blue rib-bons

Go back to the beginning and sing to the End.
(Da Capo al Fine)

That tie up my bon-nie brown hair. _____ And it's

County Fair, Grandma Moses, copyright © 1985 Grandma Moses Properties Co., N.Y.

Grandma Moses started painting when she was in her seventies. She liked to use country settings. Her paintings are colorful and lively.

● Find this rhythm pattern in the song:

Hanan and Aliza

Israeli Folk Song
Translated by Harry Coopersmith
and F. Minkoff

Verse

1. Ha - nan was a shep - herd, A - li - za a sheep.
2. Ha - nan and A - li - za, they wan - dered a - long.

They played in the mea - dow where clo - ver is deep.
He played on his flute and she bleat - ed the song.

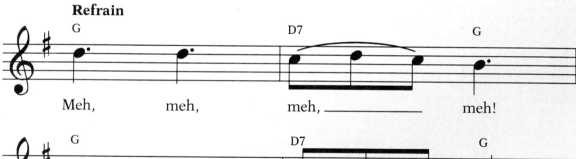

Refrain

Meh, meh, meh, _____ meh!

Beh, beh, beh, _____ beh!

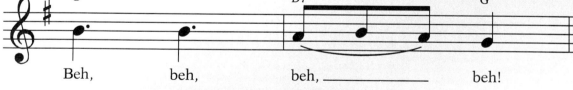

3. Hanan asked Aliza, "How are you today?"
   But all that his little Aliza could say, Meh...

4. Hanan told Aliza, "As your words are few,
   When I speak for me, I shall speak for you too!" Meh...

RONDO FORM

When people create something new, they often begin with a plan for its form. Builders plan the form of a house. Artists plan the form of a work of art. Composers plan the form of their music.

One kind of musical form is a **rondo.** In a rondo there are many sections. The first section (A) is repeated after each new section. The A section is also the last section of a rondo.

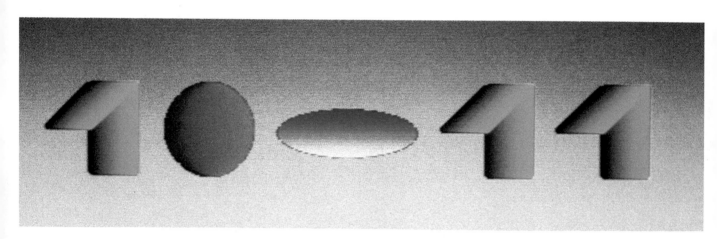

This art was made on a computer.

● Find the picture that shows a rondo form.

You can make a rondo.

● Say these words for Section A of "Our Rondo."

> We're studying musical form today,
> And this is the music for Section A.
> We'll come back right after we hear someone play.
> We're making up a rondo.

● Play the rhythm of the words of "Welcome Friends" on page 95 on a rhythm instrument for Section B.

● Say these words for Section A of "Our Rondo."

> We're studying musical form today,
> And this is the music for Section A.
> We'll come back right after we hear someone play.
> We're making up a rondo.

● Play the rhythm of the words of "Sing Together" on page 177 on a different rhythm instrument for Section C.

● Say these words for Section A of "Our Rondo."

> We're studying musical form today,
> And this is the music for Section A.
> We'll come back right after we hear someone play.
> We're making up a rondo.

The third movement of Concerto for Horn No. 3, in
E-flat Major by Wolfgang Amadeus Mozart, is a rondo.

● Listen to hear the rondo form: A B A C A.

 Allegro from Concerto for Horn No. 3, in E-flat
Major, by Wolfgang Amadeus Mozart (volf′ gang
ä-mä-dā′əs mō′ tsärt)

You heard the **French horn** in the piece by Mozart. The French horn is a very important instrument in the orchestra. It blends well with orchestral stringed instruments and woodwinds. The French horn developed from early horns made of animal horns or large seashells. The first metal horns were long and straight. Since about 1850, French horns have been made of coiled metal tubing almost twelve feet long. To change the sound the player puts one hand in the bell.

French horn mouthpiece

French horn

STRINGED INSTRUMENTS
OF OTHER LANDS

● Listen to the sound of the **balalaika** (bä-lä-lī′kä), a folk
stringed instrument played in the Soviet Union.

Minka

Russian Folk Song

1. Min-ka, Min-ka, when I leave thee, How my sad heart al-ways grieves me,
2. When I hear sweet mu-sic play-ing, Ev-'ry note to me is say-ing,

When I'm gone I long to be with Min-ka, Min-ka mine.
"Min-ka, Min-ka, fair-est maid-en, Min-ka, Min-ka mine."

When I see the full moon shin-ing, Then I will for thee be pin-ing,
When the win-ter snow is fall-ing, I must go, for love is call-ing,

Min-ka, Min-ka, fair-est maid-en, Min-ka, Min-ka mine.
Call-ing me to be with Min-ka, Fair-est Min-ka mine.

200

The balalaika is the most popular folk stringed instrument in the Soviet Union. Its body is shaped like a triangle, and it has three pairs of strings and a long neck. It is played by moving a **plectrum** or pick rapidly back and forth across one or more strings. Balalaikas are made in six different sizes and are often played in an orchestra made up of almost all balalaikas.

● Listen for the sound of the balalaika.

 Sound of the balalaika

The **ch'in** (chin) is a very old Chinese instrument. It is made of wood and has seven strings. Its shape and sound may remind you of the Appalachian dulcimer on page 54. The ch'in is laid on a table and played by sliding the fingers of one hand up and down the strings to make different pitches while the other hand plucks the strings. According to tradition, the ch'in is played by either scholars or the very wise. The ch'in is usually played without accompaniment.

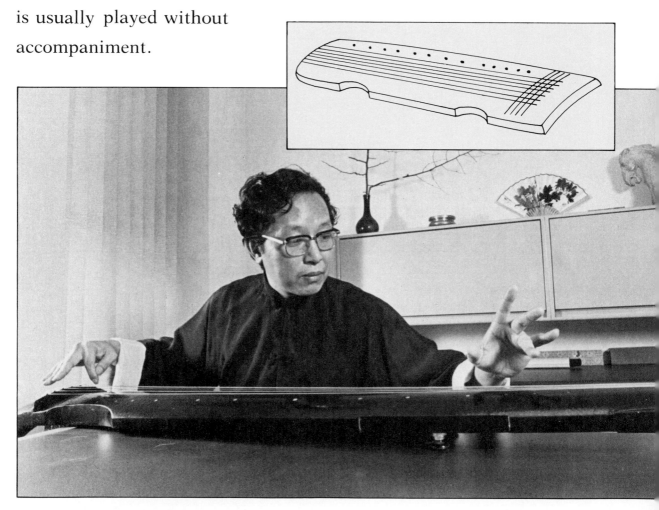

● Listen for the sound of the ch'in.

 Sound of the ch'in

The **kora** (ko'ra) is a stringed instrument from Africa. Its body is round and made from a large gourd covered with animal skin. It has several strings and is played with the fingers of both hands plucking many strings at once. The kora can have as few as five strings or as many as twenty-one. The sound of the kora is similar to that of the harp.

● Listen for the sound of the kora.

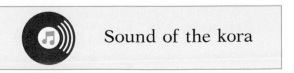

Sound of the kora

ADDING DYNAMICS

f is the symbol for loud.

What music word means loud?

p is the symbol for soft.

What music word means soft?

pp is the symbol for very soft.

What music word means very soft?

● Use one of the dynamic plans below with "Our Rondo" on page 197.

● Use your own dynamic plan with "Our Rondo."

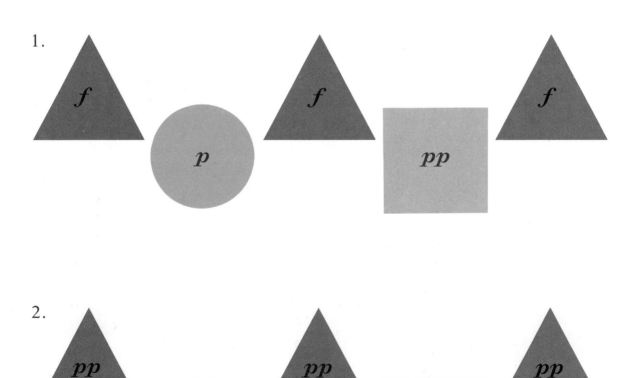

1.

2.

TEMPO

● Use a rhythm instrument to play the tempo you think each picture shows.

REVIEWING WHAT YOU'VE LEARNED

● Tell what you know about this instrument.

● Point to the instrument you hear.

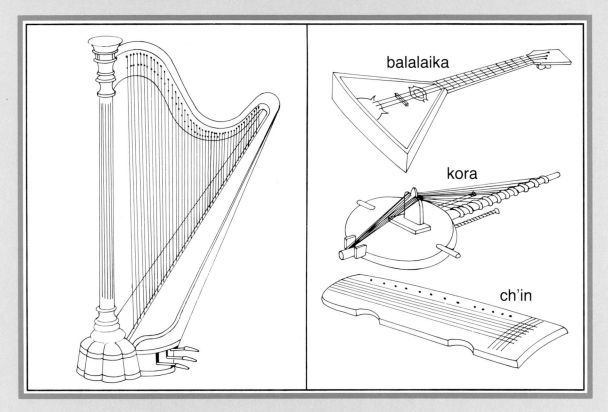

balalaika

kora

ch'in

● Match the song with the country.

"Shepherd, Shepherd"   Ghana

"Tue, Tue"   England

"Oh, Dear, What Can
   the Matter Be?"   Israel

"Hanan and Aliza"   Soviet Union

"Minka"   United States

● Sing your favorite songs.

206

JUST CHECKING

See how much you remember.

1. Which keyboard shows a whole step?

a. 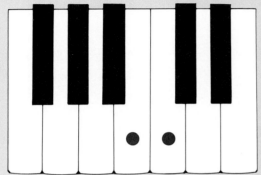   b.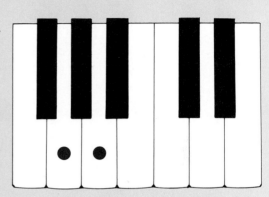

2. Give the pitch syllable or scale number for these pitches.

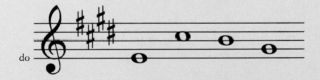

3. Which of these instruments comes from the Soviet Union?

    a. kora

    b. balalaika

    c. ch'in

4. Which of these instruments has 47 strings?

    a. ch'in

    b. harp

    c. kora

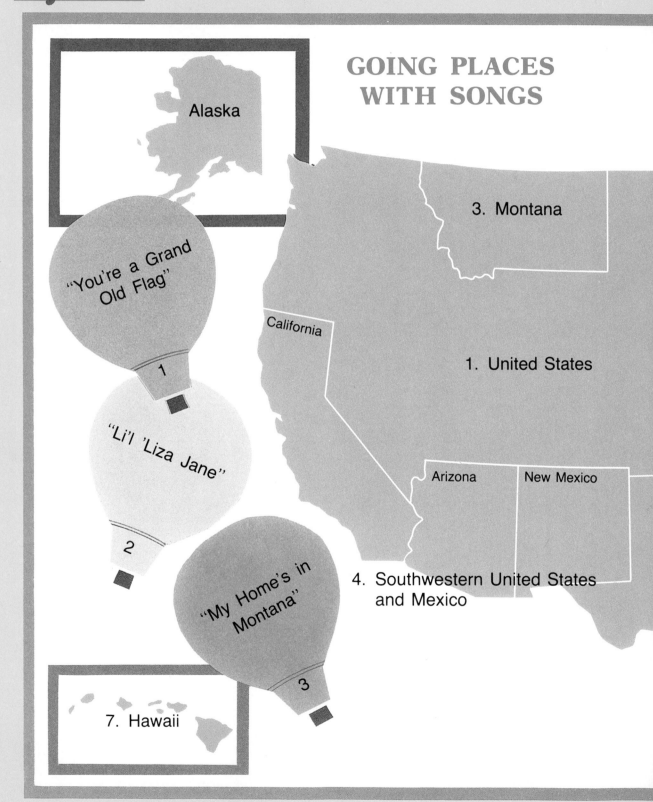

GOING PLACES
WITH SONGS

Alaska

"You're a Grand Old Flag"

1

"Li'l 'Liza Jane"

2

"My Home's in Montana"

3

3. Montana

California

1. United States

Arizona   New Mexico

4. Southwestern United States
and Mexico

7. Hawaii

- Take a balloon trip to various parts of the United States.
- Follow the balloons in order.
- Sing each song and find its place on the map.

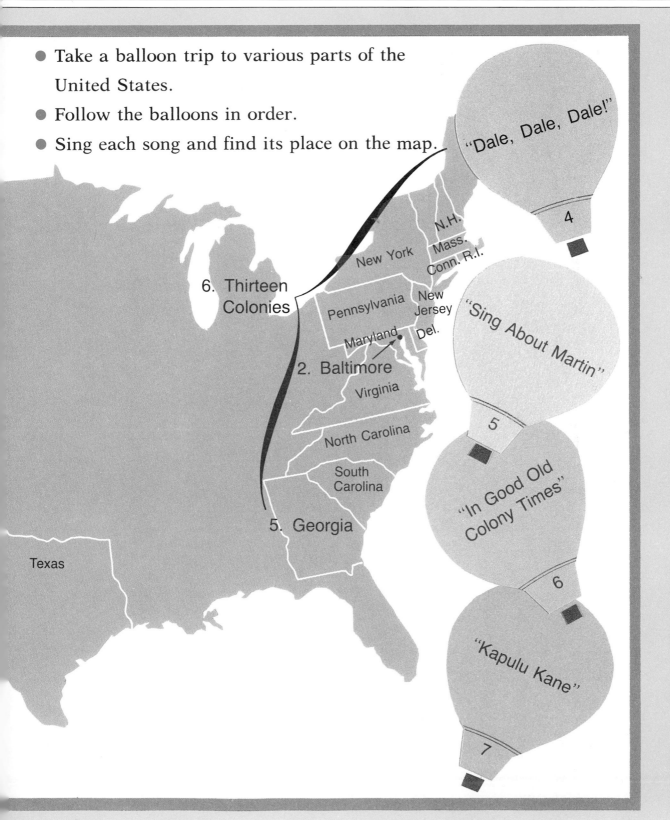

"Dale, Dale, Dale!"
4

"Sing About Martin"
5

"In Good Old Colony Times"
6

"Kapulu Kane"
7

6. Thirteen Colonies

New York
N.H.
Mass.
Conn. R.I.

Pennsylvania
New Jersey
Maryland
Del.

2. Baltimore

Virginia

North Carolina

South Carolina

5. Georgia

Texas

Stone Soup

Music, Lyrics and Script by John Horman
Adapted from the legend, "Stone Soup"

Long ago, three soldiers were returning home after a
long war. They were tired and hungry as they came to a
small village.

Song of Three Soldiers

Words and music by
John Horman

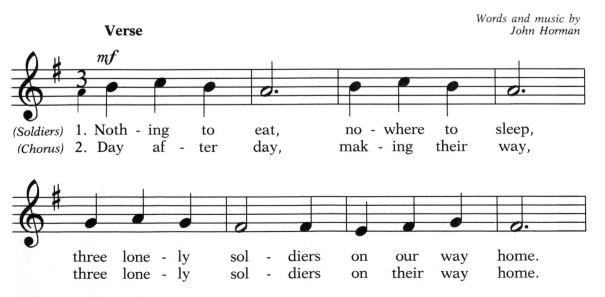

Verse

mf

(Soldiers) 1. Noth - ing to eat, no - where to sleep,
(Chorus) 2. Day af - ter day, mak - ing their way,

three lone - ly sol - diers on our way home.
three lone - ly sol - diers on their way home.

210

Ti - red are we, mar - ching just three,
In a strange place, each house and each face,

three lone - ly sol - diers on our way home. ____
three lone - ly sol - diers on their way home. ____

Refrain

Good din - ner, good bed, march on, march on!

Good din - ner, good bread, march on.

The soldiers met some of the villagers. The villagers
were not the friendly people they had been before the war.
The villagers wondered who these strange soldiers were.

Excuses, Excuses

Words and Music by
John Horman

Refrain

Soldiers

Please don't be a-larmed. We wish you no harm.

It's just that we're hun-gry and worn. ___ What we need is a bed,

some meat and some bread, we'll be up and a-way ___ by morn.

Verse

Twice as fast

Paul and Francoise   1. We wish we could help you, please lis - ten, you
Albert and Louise   2. We wish we could help you. What we speak is
The Chorus   3. They wish they could help you! It's real - ly so

must! We've had a long drought, and our
true! Our chil - dren are sick and in
sad, The war is now o - ver, They

| 1. and 2. | | 3. |

a tempo   *Soldiers*   *rit.*

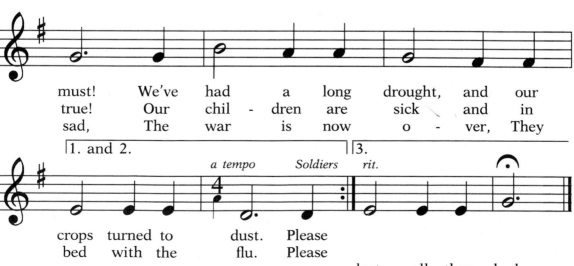

crops turned to dust. Please
bed with the flu. Please

lost all they had.

213

The villagers seemed to care only about themselves because of their troubles. The soldiers decided to tell them a secret.

The Secret

Words and Music by
John Horman

Good folk of the vil-lage, you've noth-ing to fear.

We know of your trou-bles, so be of good cheer.

We bring you a se-cret, known by but a few.

Come gath-er a-round and we'll share it with you. __

And though it sounds cra - zy, with one thing a - lone,

We'll make a fine soup from a sin - gle large stone.

It's real - ly quite sim - ple, so ea - sy to do,

From noth - ing at all we'll make won - der - ful stew! ___

The villagers couldn't believe their ears. Everyone knew that soup couldn't be made from a stone. They began to laugh and sing as they pretended to stir kettles of soup.

215

Soup from a Stone

Words and Music by
John Horman

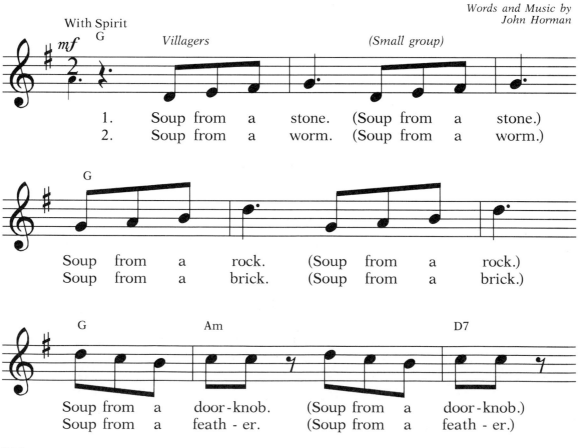

With Spirit

mf G

Villagers (Small group)

1. Soup from a stone. (Soup from a stone.)
2. Soup from a worm. (Soup from a worm.)

G

Soup from a rock. (Soup from a rock.)
Soup from a brick. (Soup from a brick.)

G   Am   D7

Soup from a door-knob. (Soup from a door-knob.)
Soup from a feath-er. (Soup from a feath-er.)

Soup from a clock. (Soup from a clock.)
Soup from a stick. (Soup from a stick.)

Soup from a fire - fly! (Soup from a fire - fly!)
Soup from an old shoe! (Soup from an old shoe!)

Soup from a bee! (Soup from a bee!)
Soup, oh so free! (Soup, oh so free!)

How ver - y dumb you must think us to be!
Why try to fool us with things that can't be!

The villagers gathered around to watch. The soldiers issued a few orders. One by one the villagers began to help.

Stone Soup
(Four part canon)

Refrain
Soldiers

Words and music by
John Horman

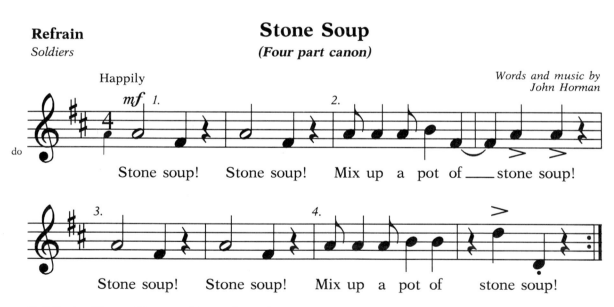

Stone soup! Stone soup! Mix up a pot of __ stone soup!

Stone soup! Stone soup! Mix up a pot of stone soup!

Soldier's Chant (Cast echoes chant.)

1. First find a kettle—
   The bigger the better! (Echo)
   Fill it with water
   The better the wetter! (Echo)

   Next build a fire
   To heat up the water. (Echo)
   Add some dry wood
   'Til the water gets hotter! (Echo)
   (Refrain by Soldiers)

2. Then boil the water
   Right to the top! (Echo)
   One large stone
   In the kettle we'll drop. (Echo)

   Good soup needs good seasoning,
   Pepper and salt. (Echo)
   This tastes much better
   Than any you've bought. (Echo)
   (Refrain by Everyone)

218

The villagers gathered around the soup pot and said,
"Taste it! Taste it! Taste it and see.
Is it the best—the best it can be?"

The soldiers tasted it and said,
"Hmmmm, well, maybe, no, no,
It needs a little . . . potato and cabbage."

A villager quickly brought one of each. Then they asked again,
"Taste it! Taste it! Taste it and see.
Is it the best—the best it can be?"

The soldiers each tasted it thoughtfully, and said,
"Hmmm, well, maybe, no, no. . .
It needs a little carrot, and onion, and parsley."

Other villagers brought these quickly and then they all said,
"Taste it! Taste it! Taste it and see.
Is it the best—the best it can be?"

The soldiers answered,
"Hmmm, well, maybe, no, no. . .
It needs a soup bone."

A villager quickly brought a soup bone and they asked their
same question again only to be answered by the soldiers,
"Hmmm, well, maybe, no, no.
It needs two more things—barley and cream."

Right away the villagers brought these.
By this time, the villagers wanted to taste the soup. It
was marvelous! They had a feast and sang and danced.

Sing a Song of Sipping Soup

Words and Music by
John Horman

Sing a song of sip-ping soup.— All a-lone or in a group.—

Find a part-ner; dance a-lone. We have made soup — from a stone!

In a cir-cle, 'round a ring,— we can dance and we can sing.—

Round and round,— to and fro,— up and down,— here we go.

To the mid-dle give a shout! We have much to sing a-bout!

Ev-ery-bod-y sing a-long, _____

Sip your soup and sing a song. _____

Sing a song of sip-ping soup. _

The next morning the whole village gave the soldiers a heroes' send-off. Now that the villagers knew how to make stone soup, they knew they would never go hungry again.

The Recipe

Partner Song No. 1 *Small Group*

Words and music by
John Horman

Stone soup! Stone soup! Mix up a pot of

stone _____ soup! Stone soup! Stone soup!

Mix up a pot of stone soup!

Stone soup! Stone soup! Stone soup!

Stone soup! Stone soup! Stone soup!

16   *mf*

The re-ci-pe's sim-ple; just start with a

stone. Then cook in a ket-tle and add a soup bone;

a dash of black pep-per, then sea-son to taste;

a small pinch of salt, there's no time to waste.

2   *f*

So add a few veg'-ta-bles, bar-ley and

cream. Then sam-ple a bit, it will taste like a dream.

Of all the in - gre - di - ents, two are a must.

One's hu-man kind-ness, the oth - er is trust.___

SONGBOOK

Up and Down

Folk Song

Up and down to earth and sky, go my po - go stick and I,

Jog - ging, spring - ing, see me fly, Hop! Hop! Hop!

Acka Backa

Playground Game

Ack - a back - a so - da crack - er, Ack - a back - a boo!

Ack - a back - a so - da crack - er, Out goes you!

Little Sally Walker

African American Singing Game

so Lit - tle Sal - ly Wal - ker, sit - ting in a sau - cer,

Cry - ing and weep - ing and look - ing for a friend.

Rise, Sal - ly, rise! Wipe your weep - ing eyes!

Turn to the east, turn to the west,

Turn to the one that you like best.

225

Name This Tune

African American Spiritual

Trampin'

African American Spiritual

I'm tramp-in', tramp-in', Tryin' to make heav-en my home.

I'm tramp-in', tramp-in', Tryin' to make heav-en my home.

Oh! The Pretty Butterflies

St. Pierre and Miquelon Folk Song

Oh! The pret-ty but-ter-flies, How they fly, how they fly.

Oh! The pret-ty but-ter-flies, How they cir-cle in the sky!

Wall Flowers

Folk Song

Wall flow-ers, wall flow-ers, grow-ing up too high,

May I get the meas-les and nev-er, nev-er die.

Go to Kath-y Tay-lor's house, she has no re-la-tions.

Tick and tack and turn your back, and kiss the con-gre-ga-tion.

227

Little Tommy Tinker

Traditional

Lit - tle Tom - my Tink - er   sat up - on   a clink - er, And

he   be - gan to   cry,   "Ma! ____   Ma!" ____

Poor   lit - tle   in - no - cent   guy.

I Lost the Farmer's Dairy Key

African American Singing Game

1. I   lost   the farm - er's dair - y key, I'm in this la - dy's gar - den.
2. A   brass key and   a   sil - ver lock, I'm in this la - dy's gar - den.

Do,   do,   let me out, I'm   in   this la - dy's   gar - den.
Do,   do,   let me out, I'm   in   this la - dy's   gar - den.

Down Came a Lady

Folk Song from Virginia

1. Down came a la - dy, down came two,
2. Down came a gentle - man, down came three,

Down came Sa - ra Ann and she was dressed in blue.
Down came Chris - to - pher as hand - some as could be.

3. Here comes a little boy, here come four,
   Here comes Pedro a-knocking at the door.

4. Up jumped Susie, up jumped Fred,
   Up jumped Timothy and he was dressed in red.

Scotland's Burning

Traditional Round

Scot - land's burn - ing, Scot - land's burn - ing, Look out, Look out,

Fire! fire! fire! fire! Pour on wa - ter, Pour on wat - er.

229

There Was a Jolly Miller

English Singing Game

There was a jol - ly mil - ler and he lived by him - self,

As the wheel went 'round he made his wealth.

One hand in the hop - per and the oth - er in the bag,

As the wheel went 'round he made his grab.

Snake Baked a Hoecake

Folk Song from Virginia

do

Snake baked a hoe-cake and set a frog to watch it,

And the frog got a nod-ding and a liz-ard came and stole _ it.

Fetch back my hoe-cake, you long-tailed nan-ny you,

Fetch back my hoe-cake, you long-tailed nan-ny, you.

America

Music by Henry Carey
Words by Samuel F. Smith

1. My coun-try, 'tis of thee, Sweet land of
2. Our fa-thers' God, to Thee, Au-thor of

lib - er - ty, Of thee I sing;
lib - er - ty, To Thee we sing;

Land where my fath-ers died, Land of the Pil-grims' pride,
Long may our land be bright With Free-dom's ho-ly light;

From ev - 'ry __ moun-tain-side Let __ free-dom ring.
Pro - tect _ us __ by Thy might, Great _ God, our King!

Children, Go Where I Send Thee

American Folk Song

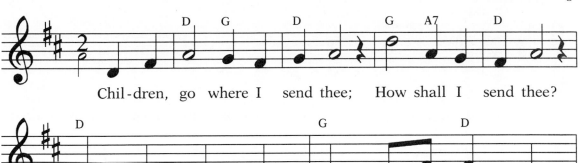

Chil-dren, go where I send thee; How shall I send thee?

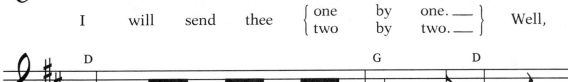

I will send thee { one by one. — / two by two. — } Well,

1. One was the lit - tle bit - ty ba - by, ___
2. Two was the Paul ___ and ___ Si - las, ___ *(Repeat 1.)*

Wrapped in swad-dling cloth-ing, _ Ly-ing in the man-ger. _

Born, born, _ oh, _ Born in Beth - le - hem. _

3. Three was the three men riding, *(repeat 2 and 1)*

4. Four was the four come a-knocking at the door, . . .

5. Five was the Gospel preachers, . . .

6. Six was the six who couldn't get fixed, . . .

7. Seven was the seven who went to heaven, . . .

8. Eight was the eight who stood by the gate, . . .

9. Nine was the nine who saw the sign, . . .

10. Ten was the Ten Commandments, . . .

233

My Valentine

Dutch Folk Song
Words by B.S.

Verse

1. I'm send-ing you a val-en-tine, val-en-tine, val-en-tine.
2. I have a se-cret val-en-tine, val-en-tine, val-en-tine.

I'm send-ing you a val-en-tine, I made it just for you.
I have a se-cret val-en-tine, and now you know it's you.

Refrain

Val-en-tine, val-en-tine, Won't you be my val-en-tine?

Val-en-tine, val-en-tine, No one else will do.

Achshav

Israeli Folk Song

Ach - shav, ach - shav, b' - E - mek Yis - r' - el.

Ach - shav, ach - shav, b' - E - mek Yis - r' - el.

Tum - ba, tum - ba, tum - ba, b' - E - mek Yis - r' - el. Hey!

Tum - ba, tum - ba, tum - ba, b' - E - mek Yis - r' - el. - el.

Amen

African American Round

A - men, A - men,

A - men, A - men, A - men.

Aiken Drum

Traditional Scottish Folk Song

Verse

1. There __ was a man lived in the moon, lived in the moon, lived in the moon.
2. And his hat was made of piz-za pie, of piz-za pie, of piz-za pie,

There __ was a man lived in the moon, And his name was Ai-ken Drum.
And his hat was made of piz-za pie, And his name was Ai-ken Drum.

Refrain

And he played a big bass fid - dle, bass fid - dle, bass fid - dle;

And he played a big bass fid - dle, And his name was Ai-ken Drum.

3. And his shirt was made of tuna fish . . .
   Refrain

4. And his pants were made of broccoli . . .
   Refrain

5. And his shoes were made of whole wheat bread . . .
   Refrain

Animal Song

Folk Song from Michigan

1. Al - li - ga - tor, hedge - hog, ant - eat - er, bear,
2. Bull - frog, __ wood - chuck, wol - ver - ine, __ goose,

Rat - tle - snake, buf - fa - lo, an - a - con - da, hare.
Whip - poor - will, chip - munk, jack - al, __ moose.

3. Mud turtle, whale, glow-worm, bat,
   Salamander, snail, Maltese cat.

Chester

Camp Song

Ches - ter, have you heard a - bout Har - ry? Just got back from the ar - my;

I hear he knows how to wear a rose, Hip, hip, hoo - ray for the ar - my.

Camptown Races

Words and Music by
Stephen C. Foster

Verse

1. Camp-town la-dies sing this song, Doo-dah, doo-dah,
2. Long tail fil-ly and the big black horse, Doo-dah, doo-dah,

Camp-town race track five miles long, Oh, doo-dah-day.
Flew the track and both cut a-cross, Oh, doo-dah-day.

Went down there with my hat caved in, Doo-dah, doo-dah.
Blind horse stick-ing in a big mud hole, Doo-dah, doo-dah.

Came back home with a pock-et ful of tin, Oh, doo-dah-day.
Could-n't touch bot-tom with a ten - foot pole, Oh, doo-dah-day.

Refrain

Goin' to run all night, Goin' to run all day,

Bet my mon-ey on the bob-tailed nag, Some-bod-y bet on the bay.

Chim Chim Cheree

Music by Richard M. Sherman
Words by Robert B. Sherman

1. Chim chim-in-ey, chim chim-in-ey, Chim chim cher-ee!
2. Chim chim-in-ey, chim chim-in-ey, Chim chim cher-ee!

A sweep is as luck-y as luck-y can be!
When you're with a sweep you're in glad com-pa-ny!

Chim chim-in-ey, chim chim-in-ey, Chim chim cher-oo!
No-where on earth is a hap-pi-er crew

Good luck will rub off when I shake hands with you.
Than those that sing "Chim chim cher-ee, chim cher-oo!"

Or blow me a kiss and that's luck-y, too.
Chim chim-in-ey, chim chim cher-ee, chim cher-oo!

Come Rowing with Me

Italian Folk Song

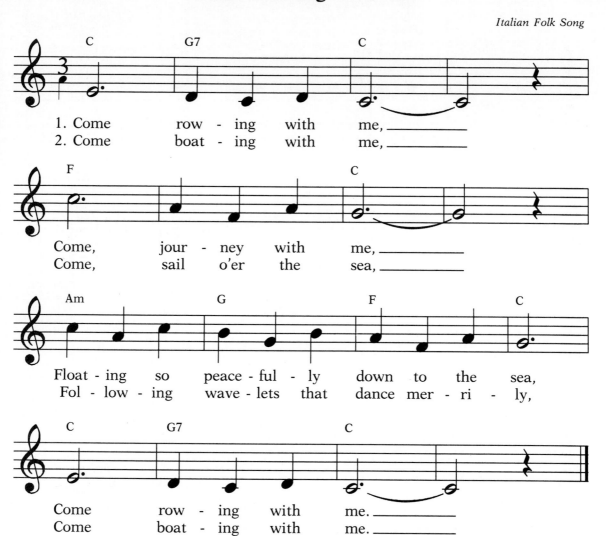

1. Come row - ing with me, _____
2. Come boat - ing with me, _____

Come, jour - ney with me, _____
Come, sail o'er the sea, _____

Float - ing so peace - ful - ly down to the sea,
Fol - low - ing wave - lets that dance mer - ri - ly,

Come row - ing with me. _____
Come boat - ing with me. _____

Cornstalk Fiddle and a Shoestring Bow

Traditional

1. I made me a fiddle and I made me a bow,
2. I tuned up my fiddle and I went to a dance.

and I learned to play the fiddle like Cotton Eye Joe.
___ I tried to make some music but I didn't get a chance.

Refrain

Corn - stalk fiddle and a shoe - string bow,
Corn - stalk fiddle and a shoe - string bow,

and if that ain't a - fiddl - in' then I don't know!
It's the very best ___ fiddle in the coun - ty - o!

3. Cotton Eye Joe lived 'cross the creek.
   He learned to play the fiddle 'bout seven days a week.
   (Refrain 1)

4. I've made lots of fiddles and made a lot of bows.
   But I never learned to fiddle like Cotton Eye Joe!
   (Refrain 2)

The Crawdad Song

American Folk Song

1. You get a line and I'll get a pole, _ hon - ey; _____
2. I sell _ craw - dads three for a dime, _ hon - ey; _____

You get a line and I'll get a pole, _ babe; _____
I sell _ craw - dads three for a dime, _ babe; _____

You get a line and I'll get a pole, And we'll go down to the
I sell _ craw - dads three for a dime, And that's a bar - gain _

craw - dad hole, _ Hon - ey, ba - by, mine. _____
an - y time, _ Hon - ey, ba - by, mine. _____

3. What will you do when the pond runs dry, honey?
   What will you do when the pond runs dry, babe?
   What will you do when the pond runs dry?
   I'll sit right down and have a cry, Honey, baby, mine.

4. Here comes a man with a sack on his back, honey;
   Here comes a man with a sack on his back, babe;
   Here comes a man with a sack on his back,
   Totin' all the crawdads he can pack, Honey, baby, mine.

5. I heard a duck say to a drake, honey;
   I heard a duck say to a drake, babe;
   I heard a duck say to a drake,
   You'll find no crawdads in this lake, Honey, baby, mine.

Crocodile Song

Traditional

She sailed a - way on a bright and sun - ny day

On the back of a croc - o - dile. "You see," said she,

"He's as tame as tame can be. I'll ride him down the Nile."

But the Croc winked his eye as she waved them all good - bye,

Wear - ing a hap - py smile. At the end of the ride,

the la - dy was in - side, And the smile was on the croc - o - dile.

Duck Dance

American Muskhogean Indian

Wee ya hay ya wee hee ya hay ya

Wee hee ya wa hay ya, wee hee ya hay ya

Wee hee ya wa hay ya, Wee hee ya hay ya. Ho ke lay ho-o-o!

For Health and Strength

Traditional Round

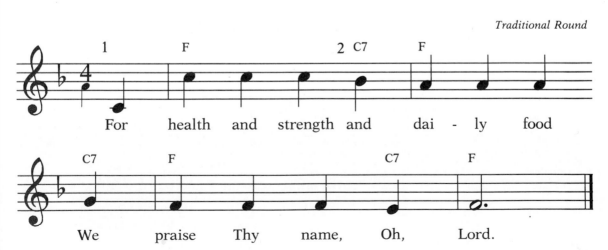

For health and strength and dai - ly food

We praise Thy name, Oh, Lord.

Garden Song

Words and Music by
David Mallett

1. Inch by inch, row by row,_ Gon-na make this
2. Pull - in' weeds and pick-in' stones,_ Man is made of

gar - den grow,_ All it takes is a rake and a hoe and a
dreams and bones, Feel the need to _ grow my _own 'cause the

piece of fer - tile ground. __ Inch by inch,
time is close at hand. ____ Grain for grain,

row by row,_ Some - one bless the seeds I sow,
sun and rain _ Find my way in na - ture's chain,

Some - one warm them from be - low _ 'til the rain comes
Tune my bod - y and my brain _ to the mu - sic

tum - bl - ing down.
from _ the land.

3. Plant your rows straight and long,
Temper them with prayer and song,
Mother Earth will make you strong
If you give her love and care.
Old crow watching hungrily
From his perch in yonder tree.
In my garden I'm as free
As that feathered thief up there.

245

Grizzly Bear

African American Song

Tell me who was the griz-zl-y, griz-zl-y bear. _

Tell me who was the griz-zl-y, griz-zl-y bear. _

Jack - o - Dia-monds was the griz-zl-y, griz-zl-y bear. _

Jack - o - Dia-monds was the griz-zl-y, griz-zl-y bear. _

Solo **D**   *Response*
He growled in the bush-es like a griz - zl - y bear. _

Solo **D**   *Response* **G**   **D**
He growled in the bush-es like a griz - zl - y bear. _

Solo **D**   *Response*
Well my { ma - ma / pa - pa } was scared of that griz - zl - y bear. _

Solo **D**   *Response* **G**   **D**
Well my { ma - ma / pa - pa } was scared of that griz - zl - y bear. _

Halleluyah

Jewish Folk Song

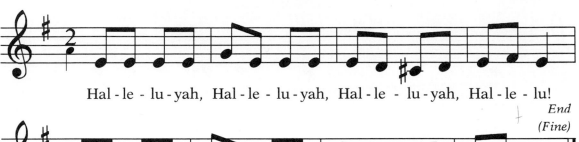

Hal - le - lu - yah, Hal - le - lu - yah, Hal - le - lu - yah, Hal - le - lu!

End
(Fine)

Hal - le - lu - yah, Hal - le - lu - yah, Hal - le - lu - yah, Hal - le - lu!

Go back to the beginning and sing to the End.
(Da Capo al Fine)

Hal - le,   Hal - le - lu - yah!   Hal - le,   Hal - le - lu - yah!

Patito

Mexican Folk Song

1. Pa - ti - to, pa - ti - to co - lor de ca - fé.
2. Me gus - ta la le - che, me gus - ta el té,

Si tú no me quier - es me quier - e Jo - sé.
Pe - ro más me gus - tan los o - jos de U - sted.

I Caught a Rabbit

Kentucky Folk Song

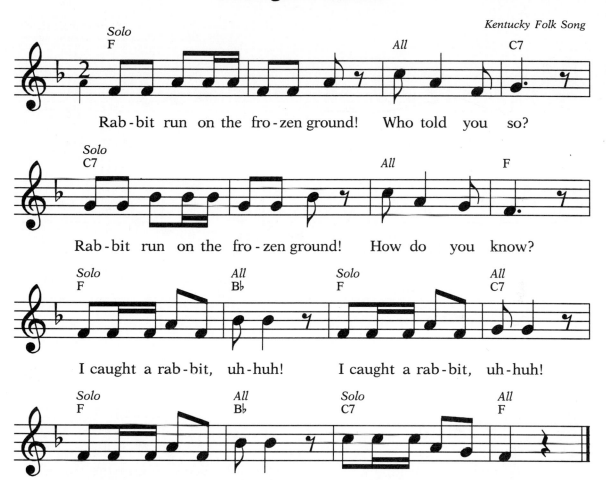

Rab-bit run on the fro-zen ground! Who told you so?

Rab-bit run on the fro-zen ground! How do you know?

I caught a rab-bit, uh-huh! I caught a rab-bit, uh-huh!

I caught a rab-bit, uh-huh! I caught a rab-bit, oh!

High Is Better Than Low

Words and Music by
Howard Dietz and Arthur Schwartz

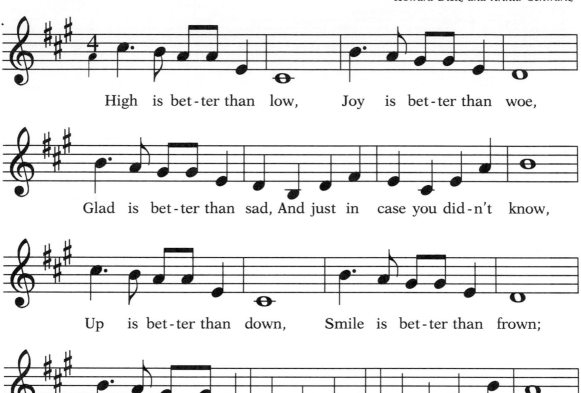

High is bet-ter than low, Joy is bet-ter than woe,

Glad is bet-ter than sad, And just in case you did-n't know,

Up is bet-ter than down, Smile is bet-ter than frown;

Don't be drag-ging a fear-ful, tear-ful face a-round the town.

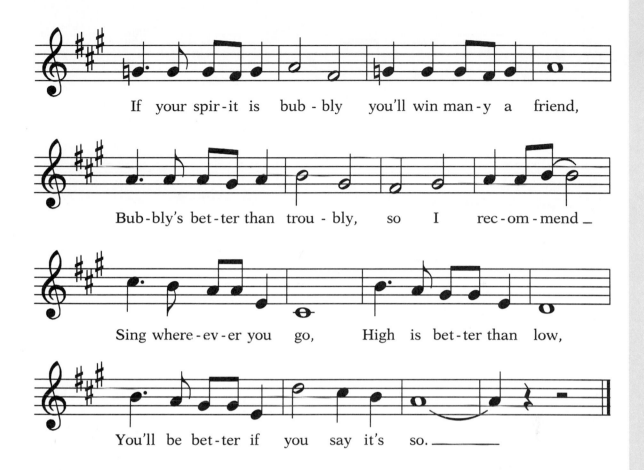

If your spir-it is bub-bly you'll win man-y a friend,

Bub-bly's bet-ter than trou-bly, so I rec-om-mend

Sing where-ev-er you go, High is bet-ter than low,

You'll be bet-ter if you say it's so.

Japanese Rain Song

Japanese Folk Song
English Translation by Roberta McLaughlin

Pit - ter, pat - ter, fall - ing, fall - ing, rain   is fall - ing down,
A - me, a - me, fur - e, fur - e, ka - a - san - ga,

Moth - er comes to bring um - brel - la, rain   is fall - ing down.
Jya - no me de o mu kae, ___ U - re shi - na.

Pi chi, pi chi, cha pu, cha pu, ran, ran, ran.

Juba

African American Folk Song

Ju - ba this and ju - ba that, Ju - ba { saw / had / found / chased } a yel - low cat,

Ju - ba up and ju - ba down, Ju - ba { run - ning / jump - ing / hop - ping / danc - ing } all a - round.

Up in a Balloon

English Folk Song
Words Adapted

1. Up in a ball - oon, boys, Up in a ball - oon, ___
2. Blast - ing off from earth, we'll rock - et in - to space, ___

Out a - mong the lit - tle stars, ___ sail - ing 'round the moon. ___
All a - long the Milk - y Way the plan - ets we will chase. ___

Up in a ball - oon, boys, Up in a ball - oon, ___ It's
Sail - ing past a com - et cir - cling 'round the moon. ___ It's

some - thing ver - y jol - ly to be up in a ball - oon. ___
some - thing ver - y jol - ly to be fly - ing 'round the moon. ___

Mama Paquita

Carnival Song from Brazil
English Words by M.S.

1. Ma - ma Pa - qui - ta, Ma - ma Pa - qui - ta,
2. Ma - ma Pa - qui - ta, Ma - ma Pa - qui - ta,

Ma - ma Pa - qui - ta has no mon - ey for pa - pa - yas;
Ma - ma Pa - qui - ta has no mon - ey for pa - ja - mas;

Can't buy pa - pa - yas, can't buy ba - na - nas;
Can't buy pa - ja - mas, can't buy som - bre - ros;

She can - not buy pa - pa - yas or ba - na - nas. No, ma - ma - ma - ma,
She can - not buy pa - ja - mas or som - bre - ros. No, ma - ma - ma - ma,

254

Ma - ma Pa - qui - ta,   Ma - ma Pa - qui - ta,
Ma - ma Pa - qui - ta,   Ma - ma Pa - qui - ta,

Ma - ma Pa - qui - ta will not have a ripe pa - pa - ya;
Ma - ma Pa - qui - ta will not have the fine pa - ja - mas;

No ripe pa - pa - ya,   no ripe ba - na - na,
No fine pa - ja - mas,   no fine som - bre - ros,

So go to Car - ni - val to laugh and dance and sing.
So go to Car - ni - val to laugh and dance and sing.

Move into Music

Words and music by Barbara Staton

1. Come on and move into music, move into music,
   Move, move, move, move,
   Move into music now!

2. Come on and clap to the music, clap to the music,
   Clap, clap, clap, clap,
   Clap to the music now!

3. Come on and snap to the music, snap to the music,
   Snap, snap, snap, snap,
   Snap to the music now!

4. Now move your knees to the music, move your knees to the music,
   Move, move, move, move,
   Move your knees to the music now!

Bridge
   Come on and move, move, move, move,
   Move, move, move, move,
   Move into music, move into music,
   Move into music now!

5. Now let's walk to the music, walk to the music,
   Walk, walk, walk, walk,
   Walk to the music now!

6. Now let's hop to the music, hop to the music,
   Hop, hop, hop, hop,
   Hop to the music now!

7. So let's move into music, move into music,
   Move, move, move, move,
   Move into music now, move into music now,
   Come on and move into music now!

Mr. Frog Went Courtin'

American Folk Song

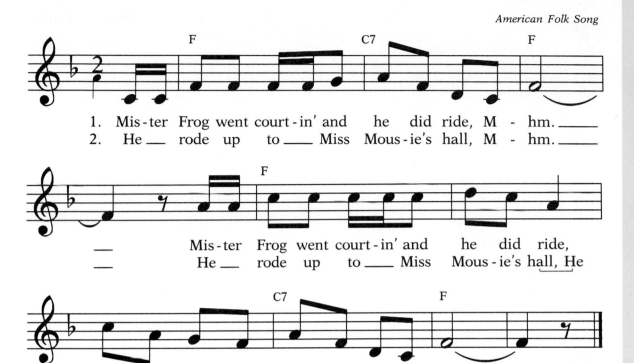

1. Mis-ter Frog went court-in' and he did ride, M - hm._____
2. He __ rode up to __ Miss Mous-ie's hall, M - hm._____

__ Mis-ter Frog went court-in' and he did ride,
__ He __ rode up to __ Miss Mous-ie's hall, He

Sword and pis - tol by his side, M - hm._____
gave a loud knock and he gave a loud call, M - hm._____

3. He took Miss Mousie on his knee, Mhm.
   He took Miss Mousie on his knee,
   He said, "Miss Mouse, will you marry me?" Mhm.

4. Miss Mousie blushed and hung her head, Mhm.
   Miss Mousie blushed and hung her head,
   "You'll have to ask Uncle Rat," she said, Mhm.

5. Next day Uncle Rat he rode to town, Mhm.
   Next day Uncle Rat he rode to town,
   To get his niece a wedding gown, Mhm.

Nani Wale Na Hala

Hawaiian Folk Song

1. Na - ni wa - le na ha - la, E - a, e - a.
2. Ke — on - i a e - la, E - a, e - a.

O Na - u - e i - ke ka - i, E - a, e - a.
Pi - li ma - i Ha - e - na, E - a, e - a.

Never Sleep Late Anymore

George Winston
Compiled by Robert Kensey
American Folk Song

Oh, just let me get up in the ear - ly morn,

Just let me get up in the ear - ly morn,

Just let me get up in the ear - ly morn

And I'll nev - er sleep late an - y - more. ____

Noah's Ark

African American Spiritual

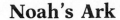

Verse

Solo F ... *Group* ... C7

1. Old No-ah built him-self an ark, one more riv-er to cross,
2. The an-i-mals came two by two, one more riv-er to cross,

Solo C7 ... *Group* ... F

And built it all of hick-o-ry bark, one more riv-er to cross.
The el-e-phant and kan-ga-roo, one more riv-er to cross.

Refrain

F Bb F ... C7 F

One more riv-er, _____ And that's the riv-er of Jor-dan;

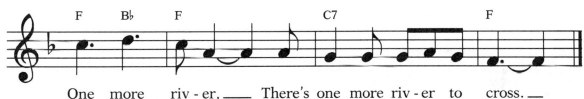

F Bb F ... C7 F

One more riv-er, _____ There's one more riv-er to cross. __

3. The animals came three by three, one more river to cross.
   The baboon and the chimpanzee, one more river to cross. *Refrain*

4. The animals came four by four, one more river to cross,
   Old Noah got mad and hollered for more, one more river to cross. *Refrain*

5. The animals came five by five, one more river to cross.
   The bees came swarming from the hive, one more river to cross. *Refrain*

6. The animals came six by six, one more river to cross.
   The lion laughed at the monkey's tricks, one more river to cross. *Refrain*

7. When Noah found he had no sail, one more river to cross,
   He just ran up his old coat tail, one more river to cross. *Refrain*

8. Before the voyage did begin, one more river to cross.
   Old Noah pulled the gangplank in, one more river to cross. *Refrain*

9. They never knew where they were at, one more river to cross.
   'Til the old ark bumped on Ararat, one more river to cross. *Refrain*

The Old Brass Wagon

American Singing Game

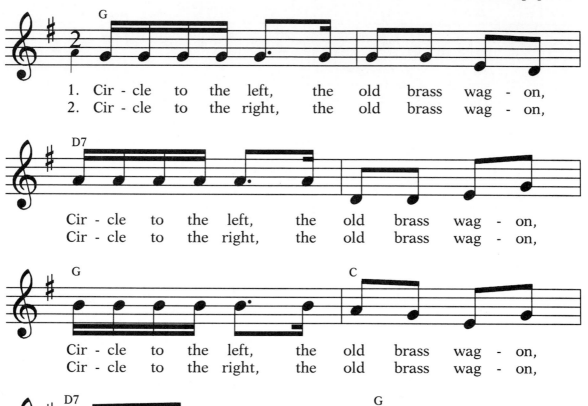

1. Cir - cle to the left, the old brass wag - on,
2. Cir - cle to the right, the old brass wag - on,

Cir - cle to the left, the old brass wag - on,
Cir - cle to the right, the old brass wag - on,

Cir - cle to the left, the old brass wag - on,
Cir - cle to the right, the old brass wag - on,

You're the one, my dar - ling.
You're the one, my dar - ling.

3. Elbow swing, the old brass wagon, (3 times)
   You're the one, my darling.

4. Promenade right, the old brass wagon, (3 times)
   You're the one, my darling.

5. Center all, the old brass wagon,
   Out to the ring, the old brass wagon,
   Center all, the old brass wagon,
   You're the one, my darling.

6. Ev'rybody swing, the old brass wagon, (3 times)
   You're the one, my darling.

Old Folks at Home

Words and music by
Stephen Foster

1. Way down upon the Swanee River, Far, far away.
    There's where my heart is turning ever,
    There's where the old folks stay.

Refrain

    All the world is sad and dreary
    Everywhere I roam;
    O lordy, how my heart grows weary,
    Far from the old folks at home.

2. All up and down the whole creation, Sadly I roam,
    Still longing for the old plantation,
    And for the old folks at home.

Refrain

Ole Tare River

American Folk Song

1. Way _ down in North Car' - li - na *(whistle)* _____
2. Now _ Nan - cy, I must leave you, *(whistle)* _____

On the banks of Ole Tare Riv - er, *(whistle)* _____
Do not let our part - ing grieve you, *(whistle)* _____

I go from there to Al - a - bam - a, *(whistle)* _____
Dance and __ sing, for - get your sor - row, *(whistle)* _____

For to see my ole Aunt Han - nah. *(whistle)* _____
I'll be back some - time to - mor - row.

261

Pity the Poor Patat

Words and Music by Josef Marais
Melody based on an African Folk Song

1. The tree, he has a bark,
2. The tree, he has his trunk,

A bark that's thick or thin.
He stares up in the sky.

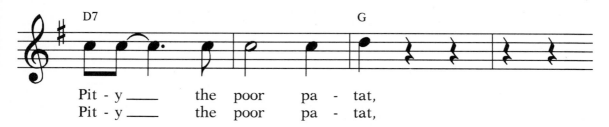

Pit - y ____ the poor pa - tat,
Pit - y ____ the poor pa - tat,

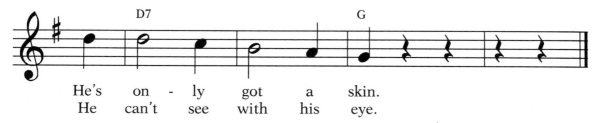

He's on - ly got a skin.
He can't see with his eye.

3. The tree, he has his leaves,
   They're waving all around.
   Pity the poor patat,
   For he lives in the ground.

4. Although the tree is proud,
   He only gives us wood.
   But from the poor patat
   We get our daily food.

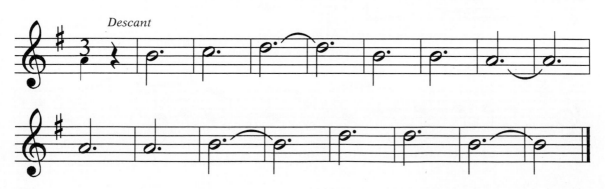

Descant

Telephone Song

American Playground Game

Hey, Char - ley! (I think I hear my name!) _

Hey, Char - ley! (I think I hear it a - gain!) _

You're want - ed on the tel - e - phone! _

(If it is - n't Ma - ry I'm not at _ home!) _

With a rick - tick - tick - e - ty tick, Oh yeh!

With a rick - tick - tick - e - ty tick, Oh yeh.

Polly Wolly Doodle

American Folk Song

1. Oh, I went down South for to see my Sal,
2. Oh, my Sal, she is a ___ maid - en fair,

Sing - ing Pol - ly Wol - ly Doo - dle all the day;
Sing - ing Pol - ly Wol - ly Doo - dle all the day;

My ___ Sal, she is a ___ spunk - y gal,
With ___ cur - ly eyes and ___ laugh - ing hair,

Sing - ing Pol - ly Wol - ly Doo - dle all the day.
Sing - ing Pol - ly Wol - ly Doo - dle all the day.

Fare thee well, fare thee well,

Fare thee well my fair - y fay,

For I'm goin' to Loui - si - an - a, For to see my Su - sy - an - a,

Sing - ing Pol - ly Wol - ly Doo - dle all the day.

There's a Hole in the Bucket

Old Dialogue Song

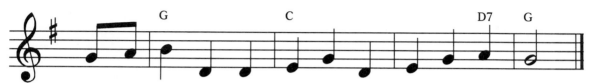

1. There's a hole in the buck - et, dear Li - za, dear Li - za,
2. Mend the hole, then, dear Geor - gie, dear Geor - gie, dear Geor - gie,

There's a hole in the buck - et, dear Li - za, a hole.
Mend the hole, then, dear Geor - gie, dear Geor - gie, the hole.

3. With _ what shall I mend it, dear Liza, dear Liza.
   With _ what shall I mend it, dear Liza, with what?

4. With a straw, _ dear Georgie, . . . a straw.

5. The _ straw is too long, _ dear Liza, . . . too long.

6. Cut the straw, _ dear Georgie, . . . the straw.

7. With _ what shall I cut it, dear Liza, . . . with what?

8. With a knife, _ dear Georgie, . . . a knife.

9. The _ knife is too dull, _ dear Liza, . . . too dull.

10. Then _ sharpen it, dear Georgie, . . . then sharpen it.

11. With _ what shall I sharpen it, dear Liza, . . . with what?

12. With a stone, _ dear Georgie, . . . a stone.

13. The _ stone is too dry, _ dear Liza, . . . too dry.

14. Then _ wet it, dear Georgie, . . . then wet it.

15. With _ what shall I wet it, dear Liza, . . . with what?

16. With _ water, dear Georgie, . . . with water.

17. In __ what shall I get it, dear Liza, . . . in what?

18. In a bucket, dear Georgie, . . . in a bucket.

19. There's a hole in the bucket, dear Liza, . . . a hole.

There Was a Crooked Man

Traditional Music
Mother Goose Rhyme

There was a crook-ed man, who went a crook-ed mile

And found a crook-ed six-pence up-on a crook-ed stile.

He bought a crook-ed cat that caught a crook-ed mouse,

And they all lived to-geth-er in a lit-tle crook-ed house.

Tideo

American Singing Game

Skip one win-dow ti - de - o, Skip two win-dows ti - de - o,

Skip three win-dows ti - de - o, Jin-gle at the win-dow ti - de - o;

Ti - de - o, ti - de - o, Jin-gle at the win-dow ti - de - o.

Tina Singu

African Folk Song

Ti - na sing - u le - lu - vu - tae - o. Wat - sha, wat - sha,

wat - sha, Ti - na, Ti - na sing - u le - lu - vu - tae - o.

Wat - sha, wat - sha, wat - sha, wat - sha.

Tinga Layo

Calypso from the West Indies
Words adapted by M.S.

Refrain

Tin - ga Lay - o! Come, lit - tle don - key, come;

Tin - ga Lay - o! Come, lit - tle don - key, come.

4. *Last time only* *End* **Verse**

Come, lit - tle don - key, come. 1. My don - key sí, my don - key
2. My don - key haw, my don - key

Go back to the beginning and sing to the End.
(Da Capo al Fine)

no, My don - key sits when I say to go.
gee, My don - key won't do a thing for me.

3. My donkey balk, my donkey bray,
   My donkey won't hear a thing I say.
   Refrain

Which Is the Way to London Town?

Music by Carroll Rinehart
Words Anonymous

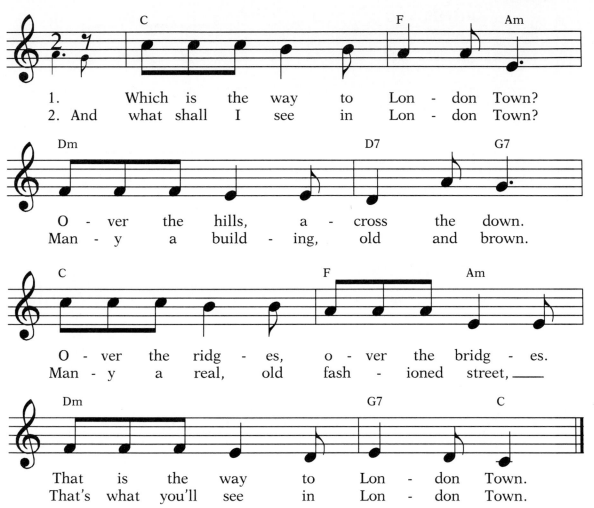

1. Which is the way to Lon - don Town?
2. And what shall I see in Lon - don Town?

O - ver the hills, a - cross the down.
Man - y a build - ing, old and brown.

O - ver the ridg - es, o - ver the bridg - es.
Man - y a real, old fash - ioned street, ___

That is the way to Lon - don Town.
That's what you'll see in Lon - don Town.

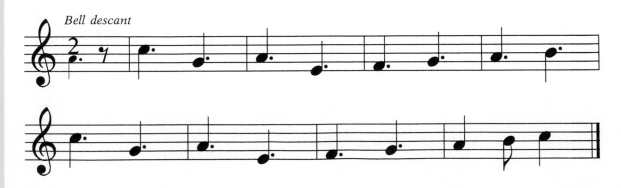

Bell descant

Wondering

Bohemian Folk Song

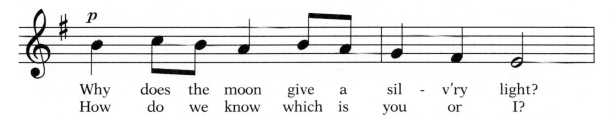

1. Where are the clouds that were here last night?
2. How far a - way is the dis - tant sky?

Why does the moon give a sil - v'ry light?
How do we know which is you or I?

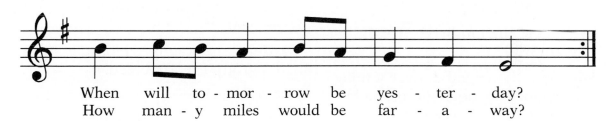

Who can tell? Who can say?
Who can tell? Who can say?

When will to - mor - row be yes - ter - day?
How man - y miles would be far - a - way?

GLOSSARY

arco to play a stringed instrument by drawing a bow across the strings, **116**

ballad a song that tells a story in which all verses are sung to the same melody, **102**

call and response a musical form in which the solo call is followed by a group response, **107**

chord three or more tones sounding together, **34**

climax a musical center of interest, **173**

coda an ending section to a piece of music, **61**

descant a second melody that sounds at the same time as the main melody, but is higher, **131**

dotted half note (𝅗𝅥.), **33**

dynamics the loudness or softness of sound, **10**

fermata (⌢) a symbol over a note that means the note should be held longer than its written value, **12**

flat (♭) a symbol that means a tone should be lowered by a half step, **184**

forte (*f*) loud, **41**

fortissimo (*ff*) very loud, **128**

fret a thin metal bar dividing the fingerboard of a stringed instrument into sections, **47**

gigue a dance, **94**

half note (𝅗𝅥), **31**

half step the distance between a pitch and the next closest pitch on a keyboard, **182**

hula a native Hawaiian dance that uses hand and body movements to tell a story, **167**

imitation music that is repeated by other voices or instruments, **109**

interlude music that is in between the main parts of a song, or longer composition, **61**

introduction music that comes before a song or other musical composition, **61**

mariachi a Mexican street band, **73**

meter beats grouped by sets in a piece of music, **50**

meter signature the symbol at the beginning of each song that tells how many beats are in each measure and the kind of note that gets one beat, **16**

pattern the way in which the notes in a group are arranged, **4**

phrase a short section of music that is one musical thought, **144**

pianissimo (*pp*) very soft, **128**

piano (*p*) soft, **41**

pizzicato to play a stringed instrument by plucking the strings with a finger, **116**

plectrum a pick used to strike the strings of some stringed instruments, **201**

quarter note (♩), **30**

refrain a section of a song that is repeated after each verse, **32**

ritard to get slower gradually, **94**

rondo a musical form in which the first section is repeated several times with a different section between each of the repeats, **196**

section a part of the whole, **11**

sharp (♯), a symbol that raises a pitch one half step, **183**

spiritual a folk song that has spiritual meaning, **106**

staff the five lines and four spaces on which music is written, **35**

tempo the speed of the beat in music,

texture the thickness or thinness of sound that results when different pitches are played or sung together, **185**

tone color the sound that is special to each instrument or voice, **36**

whole note (o), **150**

whole rest (▬), **150**

whole step the distance in pitch equal to two half steps, **182**

CLASSIFIED INDEX

LISTENING SELECTIONS

Sound of a kora, **203**

"Street Song" by Carl Orff, **127**

"The Swan" from *Carnival of the Animals* by Camille Saint-Saëns, **147**

"The Twittering Machine" by Gunther Schuller from *Seven Studies on Themes of Paul Klee*, **81**

"Variations on 'Carnival of Venice,'" by Niccolo Paganini, **119**

"Voiles" from *Preludes*, Book 1, by Claude Debussy, **23**

"Waltz of the Flowers" from *The Nutcracker*, by Peter Ilyich Tchaikovsky, **78, 180**

ALPHABETICAL SONG INDEX